UNRESTRAINED
CREATIVITY

HOW SANDLOT BASEBALL CAN UNLEASH CREATIVITY FOR KIDS IN THE TECH AGE

DR. SHAFER H. ZYSMAN

Copyright © 2025 Dr. Shafer H. Zysman.

All rights reserved. No part of this book may be reproduced, stored, or transmitted by any means—whether auditory, graphic, mechanical, or electronic—without written permission of both publisher and author, except in the case of brief excerpts used in critical articles and reviews. Unauthorized reproduction of any part of this work is illegal and is punishable by law.

ISBN: 979-8-89419-604-6 (sc)
ISBN: 979-8-89419-605-3 (hc)
ISBN: 979-8-89419-606-0 (e)

Because of the dynamic nature of the Internet, any web addresses or links contained in this book may have changed since publication and may no longer be valid. The views expressed in this work are solely those of the author and do not necessarily reflect the views of the publisher, and the publisher hereby disclaims any responsibility for them.

One Galleria Blvd., Suite 1900, Metairie, LA 70001
(504) 702-6708

DEDICATION

In memory of my parents, Majer and Rachel Zysman.
Their encouragement and love enabled me to be myself.
My late brother, Jerry, who took me to my first
Major League Baseball Game.

CONTENTS

DEDICATION iii

ACKNOWLEDGEMENTS vii

INTRODUCTION xi

CHAPTER 1: THE EXPERIENCE 1

CHAPTER 2: WATCHING THE BOUNCING BALL: THE STAGES OF THE CHILD ATHLETE'S DEVELOPMENT 14

CHAPTER 3: CREATIVITY: PLAYING THE DREAM 28

CHAPTER 4: FROM STREET FREE PLAY TO CYBER PLAY 45

CHAPTER 5: CAN I BE INCLUDED? THE SPECIAL NEEDS EXPERIENCE 60

CHAPTER 6: THE GREAT DIVIDE 75

CHAPTER 7: OBESITY: NO TIME TO SIT ON THE BENCH..........90

CHAPTER 8: AVOID THE BASEPATH OF SLIDING INTO ALCOHOL AND DRUGS.........105

CHAPTER 9: STAY IN THE BATTER'S BOX.....125

CHAPTER 10: CHOOSING ACADEMICS, SPORTS, OR BOTH................132

CHAPTER 11: SANDLOT BASEBALL IN LATIN AMERICA AND A TICKET TO CLIMBING OUT OF POVERTY...................137

CHAPTER 12: DREAM TO THE MAJOR LEAGUES................143

CHAPTER 13: FOUL BALL: PARENTS PLAYING BEHIND THE FOUL LINE................159

CHAPTER 14: THE HOME OF GENERATIONS......................169

CHAPTER 15: THE WINDUP............................182

REFERENCES.......................191

ABOUT THE AUTHOR.................203

ACKNOWLEDGEMENTS

Writing a book is a team effort. It requires ongoing encouragement and support. Honestly, this book has been under construction for 20 years. There were many times while writing the manuscript that I obviously slacked, procrastinated, and doubted myself. It was sitting on a shelf, waiting patiently for its time to become whole.

Without the input of family, friends, professional baseball players, a group of Librarians, and publication staff, this book could have taken another decade to complete or may have never been completed.

Specifically, I appreciate the many questions and hours that librarians have offered me in researching the multiple issues covered in the ensuing chapters. This includes the assistance of the professional staff at the Research Department at the National Baseball Hall of Fame, Stony Brook University Library, and The New York City Public Library System.

It was humbling for a relatively new author to reach out to professional baseball players and receive a response and encouragement. I could have simply been a fan reaching out for an autograph or something of that nature, but that was not my goal. I legitimately wanted their insights regarding child development and baseball, which they recognized and obliged to me inquires. Among them includes that gracious letter I received from the Yogi Berra Museum and Learning Center and Tommie Lasorda, along with interviews with Bobby Thompson, Jon Matlack, and Bud Harrelson. I thank them for sharing their experiences and for promoting knowledge as well as describing their unique journeys to the Major Leagues.

The editors and promoters of the publishing staff at Penguin Book Writers, especially Jane Foster, who was my project coordinator. When I shared my story and barriers toward finishing this book, one said, "that is what we are here for. We will help you make it happen." They laid out a schedule and a plan, and a dormant project became a reality.

I would be remiss to leave out the many friends and teammates that played baseball with me as a kid and even into my mid-50s. There were many who tolerated my errors, strikeouts, and my glorious moments on the field. I would need another book to name them all. Thank you all for the memories, and it was those experiences that I reflect on in the various chapters ahead.

The spirit of freestyle sports playing is still an intrinsic part of my weekly routine. I have played Basketball with a small core of guys for over 25 years. They inspire me on the court and are wondering when are they finally going to read the book. Andy Weisburg, Steve Vacarcarelli, Jules Mencher, and the many other players at the Suffolk JCC, it's here.

I honor my patients when learning of my book project would start a session by saying, "Hey Doc, I have an idea for you! Your thoughts were heard and seriously considered. Thank you for your input."

Friendship foments conversations and offers alternative perspectives on issues. Close family friends have often engaged in that process and have accompanied me to baseball games where we simply have good times. Undoubtedly, they deserve mentioning: my pals, Steven Askinas, Robert Kronrad, Gary Miller and James Baer.

My friends and colleagues have collaborated with me in treating many patients over the years, specifically Ann Defilippo and Anthony Zeffiro. Anthony consistently texted me book title ideas, and finally, I was able to choose one that fits. Ann told me many stories of her family's love for baseball that inspired me to take the early drafts of the manuscript off the shelf and finally complete it.

Of course, my family who I love dearly. I want to thank my sons, Marc, and Jeffrey for the initial spark. When they were kids their youthful, spontaneous play ignited an idea that is now shared publicly.

My wife, Rae, who is always creating great paintings, taught me that self-expression through an art form leads to extraordinary personal growth and a social contribution that can be appreciated by many.

INTRODUCTION

I love baseball. The sport has been part of my life since early childhood and still has a presence in my senior years. It became important because when I first played on sandlot fields. I, along with my neighborhood friends, had to think creatively, outside of the box. A rock or a piece of wood lying around was transformed into bases which composed the playing field. Old beaten up, shriveling, weathered balls or rubber Spalding balls were our baseballs. Very few of us could afford to buy a new shiny white, perfectly red-stitched ball.

Baseball requires multiple players. It brought the neighborhood kids to an unoccupied lot where we gathered to have fun and make friends. We learned to be non-judgmental of the talented versus weaker players - all accepted here! We learned to be spontaneous. We experienced winning and losing together, all remaining pals before and after the game. These were lessons in life that transcended the playing field.

This book is not exclusively about baseball or a typical book on sports. The underlying focus is to understand the significance of how children use sports as a social means to foster creativity, self-esteem and develop individual identities. It follows a series of a child's psychological and social developmental phases that impact his or her growth as individuals.

The initial impetus for this book was simply watching my sons playing with school friends in my backyard. These were kids that were not very athletically talented but were having a great time running and laughing with each other by playing free style. It certainly brought back my personal childhood memories with the realization that this method of play appears to be waning, a growing phenomenon that needs serious attention.

Nowadays, fewer children go out and play with their friends spontaneously. Many kids are not playing with neighbors on the streets or are out in vacant neighborhood ball fields to play a game of pick-up baseball and other sports. Their lives are planned with scheduled activities and their engagement with sports is channeled through structured play, such as organized little league teams. These teams have great value to a child's growth experiences, but they have inherent limitations.

Parental over-involvement in orchestrating a child's daily social and play routine, can impede a child's selfexpression, problem-solving abilities. Social awareness and judgment. Learning evolves from allowing a child to make mistakes as opposed to expecting perfection and protection. Excessive adult intervention on a child can backfire with respect to a child's path toward maturity and Independence.

In 43 years of practice in psychoanalysis, family therapy, and addictions, I received multiple calls from parents who wanted their children treated. These parents expressed feelings of helplessness when describing that their kids are suffering from anxiety, depression, and alcohol/drug abuse.

Doctor, what can I do? My child's grades are falling. They are avoiding meals with the family. He spends endless hours in his room, and I cannot get my son to respond to me. My family is hurting. Many factors contribute to this disconnect between children and parents in addition to being alienated from others.

Increasingly, the rise of social media, including cyber play, is resulting in social isolation amongst today's youths. It is a form of avoidance, escape and separation from parental control. Street play has been transformed into kids networking out of their bedrooms. Its stifling creativity and maturity. It restrains the process of forming healthy social relationships. This alarming trend is a sign that we are amid a mental health pandemic.

This book is historically relevant to our changing norms. The ensuing chapters will discuss and demonstrate how our society, with the help of parents and other influential adults in concert with their children can begin to change the trend of social isolationism and symptoms associated with this phenomenon. It intertwines talking baseball and an analysis of a child's maturation process.

One chapter also looks at the issue of special needs children and their struggles in being integrated into sports - a subject rarely broached in most sports literature.

Another chapter provides testimonials from professional ballplayers who share their thoughts on sandlot and team sports.

It would be remiss to exclude comments from family members who receive uplifting feelings from watching their loved ones playing baseball. Certainly, examining the intergenerational bonding experience that baseball has on the players and their families. A chapter is devoted to sharing these insights.

As kids, as parents, as mentors and as a society, we are at a critical juncture. We are moving away from freestyle play and are encouraged to partake in planned interactive activities. The impact can be significant in the development of a child's creative and self-motivating skills. This book helps everyone in the family to evaluate and comprehend how it impacts them individually. Play is more than a kid's game; it's an individual's script in advancing emotional, physical, spiritual, and social growth.

Dr. Shafer H. Zysman
Nissequogue, New York

CHAPTER 1

THE EXPERIENCE

Creativity is metamorphous of mental massaging. The child athlete exercises the brain's thought processes to stimulate new thoughts and ideas. In various professional fields, this process is part of the practice. For instance, in the field of analytical psychology, the process of free association is a creative method that brings together emotional experiences and thoughts. The traditionally associated analytical couch found in the office creates the environmental medium and mood to enhance the creative process.

In boardrooms, members of a corporate team meet together to brainstorm new ideas. The free-flowing chemistry of the boardroom brainstorming meetings invites new, creative, and problem-solving solutions. The idea is to minimize structure and specific role definition to accentuate the spontaneity of new ideas.

For kids, what accelerates new ideas and creative thoughts depends largely on the kind of activities and environment they grow up in. Take the sandlot experience, for example. The sandlot is more than just a vacant ground where children 'casually go and hang out' with other kids. The impact it has on a child's cognitive, psychosocial, motor, linguistic, and emotional skills is massive. It allows the child athlete to be creative and physical. It plays a significant part in raising a creative, confident, and happy child. The basic rules of the game provide rudimentary boundaries, but the play itself is an experiential and self-searching activity. In the sandlot game, every child athlete is good enough to play. Every player is able to perform at an individual pace and to the best of his ability. Each player is a hero. There is no structured grading of performance, which may exclude or limit the playtime for so-called mediocre or poor players.

In recent years, the community sandlot experience is gradually becoming a phenomenon of the past. More communities throughout the United States have sponsored organized league play. The child athlete can join a team at the age of five. This may sound great at first. We are led to believe that our child is getting a platform that will recognize his talents at a very young age. We dream of future opportunities that might cross our child's path as he'll perform in the organized leagues. We might get so carried away at the thought of such platforms that we fail to think of the cons that come with them. The old glory of playing eventually transforms into the glory of just being on the team and playing part of the time.

Don't get me wrong. I'm all for structured games and the opportunities it offers. There are, however, many reasons why I staunchly support free play for kids instead of structured games. One of these reasons stems from my own childhood experience. As a child, I have fond memories of the unorganized games I played in the sandlot. I recall it as the best part of my childhood not only because it was loads of fun, but because of the realization that came to me many years later.

Today, I often see kids without friends, sitting alone, not interacting with other kids their age, and being shy when introduced to new people. As a father of two, and as a professional in the field of mental health, I have experienced and treated problems faced by kids in today's culture. As a person who also had a childhood inspired by sports, I can understand the absence of athletic activities for a child in forming their character and values. The evolution of time has brought about some changes that are ever so evident now. Back in my days, outdoor games was a norm for children. Today, that has been replaced by cyber play. The outbreak of a pandemic that further confined people to their homes further hindered free play, causing isolation and loneliness among the young ones.

Baseball – The Nostalgic Sport of My Childhood

The part of any sports enthusiast is to expose oneself to experience the history of the sport. Hall of Fame museums have been developed over the years to blend history and the emotional connection to the sport.

Back in the day, the Baseball Hall of Fame in Cooperstown, New York, showed an orientation movie. The film begins, taking you to an open farmland area. The time of day takes place near sundown. A mother of a young player shouts out, "Tommy! It's time for dinner!" Tommy is so absorbed in the baseball game that he is playing with his friends that he cannot hear his mother's dinner call.

She continues to repeat herself, but gets no response from Tommy.

The image portrayed in the film arouses the inner core of a child's passion for playing baseball. You envision a child having great fun with his friends, expressing his emotions in a productive, cultural manner, and simply being and exploring himself.

Whenever I watch this film, this specific scene triggers my own childhood memories of this game. I can recall many nights after school and in the summer playing baseball on the empty lots along the streets of New York City, where my mother came searching for me to have dinner and do my homework. I would shout back, "We're in the seventh inning, mom. The game will be over soon." In fact, the game would go on for several more hours. My mother might have been worried to death that I would grow up to be malnourished or I would forever flunk every subject when in reality, I was having the greatest time of my life. I was being myself. At times, I pretended that I was Mickey Mantle batting in the ninth inning of the seventh game of the World Series, hitting a home run and winning the World Championship. I could also see my friends playing in the field, thinking that they were Willie Mays, Jackie Robinson, Duke Snider, and Sandy Koufax, who were determined to suppress my heroic dream.

Over the years, Hollywood producers have attempted to capture the same image. Kevin Costner's Field of Dreams and Bull Durham, Billy Crystal's, 61, and a host of other films reflect how a passion for baseball brings together a dream and social connection. This experience begins in the basic let's-get-together-and simply-play-our-hearts-out game that gives rise to great compassion and cultivates creativity for the child athlete.

As opposed to free play, organized team play accentuates winning. In sports, the object is to win. Team playoffs are introduced at an early age. Certainly, winning a game, a series, or a championship is exhilarating, euphoric, and often associated with the feeling of being in heaven on earth. The winner is faultless, makes few mistakes, and takes full advantage of the flaws of others. They are winning machines. The winning team is celebrated by earning a special trophy. This stoic image, in my view, is the antithesis of creativity. For this group, winning is a job, not simply winning for fun. The weaker players become discouraged and numbs their spirit of the game.

In the early age team concept, parents become as much a part of the system of play as the child athlete. You can spectate any given game and find a parent expressing disappointment that their son made an error or that his playtime was limited by the coach. Some parents suspect that the coach bypassed their child in the lineup to insert their own son. On occasion, the competition amongst the adults is fiercer than the child athletes playing on the field. The child's needs are compromised. He finds few opportunities to be self-initiating and creative.

The development of creativity cannot be suppressed. It is a process that develops its own life cycle. Early adult intervention in the creative process can be mustered if supported and suppressed if controlled. The sandlot is the ball field experience where the budding athlete unearths raw, unadulterated talents. It can take months and years for the raw talent to develop before it can be properly harnessed in an organized fashion.

Now, just imagine. Sandlot baseball is comparable to sitting back, visualizing a 97 mile/hour fastball being thrown wildly to home plate. The catcher has to stretch to his utmost extremities to catch the ball. The pitcher throws several more 90-plus mile/hour pitches as wildly and walks two batters an inning. Would you want this player on your team if you were hoping to win a world championship? I would. That player who owned this raw talent and demonstrated this wildness was Nolan Ryan in his early career. Ryan was a member of the 1969 miracle

World Championship New York Mets, a Hall of Famer with the all-time season strikeout record and a remarkable lifetime 7 no-hitters in his career.

Baseball is a generic experience. It has an individualized meaning for anyone that becomes exposed to the game. It is played in the mind, in the heart, and in the soul. It guides the everyday life of the individual. It is a lifelong passion that is beautifully captured in a poem by Greg Hall, a baseball fan. Hall writes:

> Baseball is grass, chalk, and dirt displayed the same yet differently
> In every park that has ever heard the words play ball.
> Baseball is a passion that bonds and divides all those who know it.
> Baseball is a pair of hands stained with newsprint, A set of eyes squinting to read a box score,
> A brow creased in an attempt to recreate a three-hour game
> From an inch square block of type.
> Baseball is the hat I wear to mow the lawn.
> Baseball is a simple game of catch and the never-ending search for the perfect knuckleball.

Baseball is Willie vs Mickey, Gibson vs Koufax, and Buddy Biancalana vs the odds.

Baseball links Kansan and Missourian, American and Japanese,

But most of all father and son.

Baseball is the scent of spring,

The unmistakable sound of a double down the line,

And the face of a 10-year-old emerging from a pile of bodies

With a worthless yet priceless foul ball.

Baseball is a language of very simple words that tell unbelievably magic tales.

Baseball is three brothers in the same uniform on the same team for one brief summer

Captured forever in a black and white photo on a table by the couch.

Baseball is a glove on a shelf, oiled and tightly wrapped,

Slumbering through the stark winter months. Baseball is a breast pocket bulging with a transistor radio.

Baseball is the reason there are transistor radios.

Baseball is a voice in a box describing men you've never met,

In a place you've never been, doing things you'll never have the chance to do.

Baseball is a dream that you never really give up on.

Baseball is precious.

Baseball is timeless. Baseball is forever.

There are several reasons why baseball became my most favorite sport over the years. It's a team sport that offers many benefits to young athletes beyond just physical fitness.

I believe that the development of a child athlete through baseball not only involves learning the rules of the game and developing their skills on the field, but it also helps them develop important social skills that can help them in their personal and professional Lives. One of the most significant benefits of baseball as a team sport is the opportunity for children to communicate with their peers. The game requires constant communication among players to coordinate plays, make adjustments, and strategize during the game. This constant communication helps children develop their social skills and improve their ability to work with others towards a common goal. As a result, children who participate in baseball are often better able to communicate their thoughts and ideas effectively and collaborate with others in various situations.

As a kid myself, I remember how my friends and I spent a great deal of time choosing sides and negotiating rules. I liked thinking about the game and making quick decisions based on what was happening on the field. When children are given the responsibility to organize themselves into teams, it provides them with a sense of autonomy and ownership over the game. They learn to negotiate rules with one another and develop a sense of fairness and justice. These skills can translate into other areas of their lives, such as negotiating with classmates or siblings, making compromises, and understanding different perspectives. Through shared experiences on the field, children learn to communicate effectively, support one another, and work towards a common goal. I recall instances when my team coordinated strategies, executed double plays, or celebrated a well-executed play. These moments fostered a sense of camaraderie and instilled in me the importance of collaboration and unity in achieving success. Moreover, baseball offers children the opportunity to develop leadership skills. As a child, I remember taking turns as the captain of my team, where I had to make decisions, motivate my teammates, and lead by example.

These experiences allowed me to cultivate leadership qualities such as communication, decision making, and responsibility. Learning to lead and guide others on the field prepared me for future leadership roles in school and beyond.

Baseball also offers a sense of community for children. The team environment provides a safe and supportive space for children to connect with others who share a common interest. This sense of community can be particularly important for children who may feel isolated or lonely in other areas of their lives. Baseball offers a sense of belonging, and children can form lasting friendships that extend beyond the boundaries of the game.

Another essential benefit of baseball as a team sport is the opportunity for children to overcome loneliness and isolation. Through teamwork, children learn to rely on one another, develop trust, and work together towards a common goal. This sense of shared responsibility can help children feel less alone and more connected to the world around them.

Finally, baseball is a game that provides children with a sense of accomplishment and self-confidence. As a child, when I used to hit a home run or made a great catch in the outfield, I felt proud of myself and it gave me a boost of self-esteem. Each player, regardless if he's good or not at the game, has a role to play, and each contribution is valued. When children are encouraged and supported, they are more likely to develop a sense of self-worth and confidence that can help them succeed in other areas of their lives.

Baseball, or any other free play in general, must be highly encouraged for kids from an early age because it not only builds physical strength but also instills emotional development by teaching them how to deal with failure, manage stress, and handle the competition.

CHAPTER 2

WATCHING THE BOUNCING BALL: THE STAGES OF THE CHILD ATHLETE'S DEVELOPMENT

The process of the development of the child athlete is incremental. It is conceptualized into four distinct stages: Awareness, Creativity, Experimentation, and Mastery. This process parallels the progression toward individuation. Individuation is defined as a maturing process that follows specific steps toward the gradual separation from a parent. This process establishes the child's individual identity. The formation of the identity correlates with various tasks that a child masters as he matures toward adulthood.

These various tasks have more to do with a child's physical activities. Acquiring technical and tactical skills, developing psychological skills (like anxiety reduction and mental strength), gaining agility and physical strength are factors that enable them to progress at their own pace. With this in mind, we need to ascertain that children are given the necessary time to develop such a skill set.

Growing up, we embrace slogans of "Be yourself" or "Don't let anything stand in your way." These messages motivate us in multiple ways. It encourages us to convert dreams into reality. It provides us a sense that we are accepted irrespective of individual characteristics; we are free to voice our opinions and capable of contributing to shaping our world. This is one of the many benefits that come with sports, and if such exposure is given at any earlier stage in life, then a child starts to progress efficiently toward the process of individuation.

1. Awareness

The essence of human development is for an individual to be him or herself. As a democratic culture, we cherish our ability to be free and independent in expressing our beliefs. These cultural expressions point to the essence of our society. We cherish our freedom. We resist excessive interference by an authority figure or institution that potentially impairs our right to free expression.

But the child's voyage toward independence involves many small creative steps. The child learns to walk before he develops his own style of running. The child learns to use his hands to shape objects before using Play-Doh to create objects and so forth.

In baseball, the child learns basic concrete concepts. He first recognizes that a bat is used for hitting before he picks it up to swing. The glove is used by fielders to catch the ball. There are bases that highlight the different running areas of the baseball diamond. Early exposure by sharing observational experiences with parents on television or observing other children playing the game accounts for the early awareness stage. This stage marks the beginning of the child athlete's movement toward becoming an independent player.

This basic premise draws from scholars who have offered a host of interpretations about the process of human development. Although there have been many positions espoused, there is a general consensus that the basis of human development is to encourage individuality and to be an active participant in their environment.

As in most scholarly debates, various views, sometimes congruent and conflictual, are offered on the fine points relative to the subject.

Mahbub Haq, a political scientist, perceives human development in a four-component paradigm: 1) equity, 2) sustainability, 3) productivity, and 4) empowerment. He defines equity as equitable access to opportunity. This differs from the concept of equality, which implies the same treatment for all people. Equity, on the other hand, is more about recognizing people who face unequal opportunities (which may perhaps be because of various disadvantages pertaining to their socio-economic status or other reasons). It ensures impartiality, justice, and fairness among all by incorporating the notion of distributive justice.

Haq perceives sustainability, the second principle, as a basic standard of well-being preserved and transferred among generations. He uses this term to refer to different spheres of life like financial, social and political. He believes respect and cultural liberty are significant to spread diversity and to build a socially sustainable development.

Thirdly, productivity is a stage when individual and economic goals are achieved by investing in people as opposed to buying innovative machines and other inanimate objects. He considers productivity as an instrumental factor of human fulfillment, varying from basic (nourishment, literacy, clothing) to complex (affording luxuries, being able to follow their dreams). Both complex and basic impact different dimensions of life. When people's needs are met, they are motivated to increase productivity by being well-nourished and facilitated. Productivity is important not only for economic growth but also for social development as it enables people to participate in economic activities, earn a livelihood, and improve their standard of living.

Finally, Haq's fourth component of human development, empowerment, is about giving people the capability to make choices and participate in decision-making processes that affect their lives. Empowerment is crucial for sustainable and equitable development as it enables individuals and communities to take control of their lives and shape their own future. It involves providing access to education, health care, political participation, and other opportunities that enhance people's capacity to make informed decisions and improve their wellbeing.

In a nutshell, Haq's paradigm of human development emphasizes the interdependence of these four components - equity, sustainability, productivity, and empowerment - in achieving sustainable and equitable development that enhances people's wellbeing and quality of life.

The seminal work of Piaget (1932) highlights that the child's early play experience is egocentric, particularly between the ages of 2/12 to 7. The child engages in play activities for fun. Competition is de-emphasized. The play experience is centered on awareness and cooperation. The child has the ability to interpret rules without rigid conformity. In fact, play rules can be tailored to accommodate the skills and cognitive abilities of the respective players.

Margaret Mahler, a child psychiatrist, studied the separation-individuation process in toddlers. She strongly argues that a child begins to separate from the caregiver at the age of two. The child explores the world, makes efforts at individuality, and runs back to the mother when he perceives the world to be anxiety-provoking. In time, the child becomes more familiar with the environment, and the time spent away from the caregiver increases.

Theories espoused by Mahler and others clearly demonstrate that awareness of the environment or "the game" is critical to the advancement of the child-athlete. The child needs to know the basic concepts of the baseball game. He needs to be aware that the game has a pitcher, first baseman, catcher, and other positions. He needs to be cognizant of the fact that a ball and bat are used to play the game. He needs to know that he must hit the ball to score a run. The rudimentary awareness of the game is derived from the repetition of observations over time (OSTROM, 1984).

Awareness is an individual process. It begins when the child observes an activity that is replayed. The child athlete's familiarity with the game of baseball begins when he constantly sees it being played on television, sandlot fields, blacktop surfaces, and neighborhood baseball diamonds. Awareness is a rudimentary step forward for the child athlete's development.

Consider the following example to understand the Awareness Stage:

The family finished their dinner. The father retreats to the den, and the child to his playroom. While the child plays with his favorite toys, he overhears the television from the den tuned into the Mets-Dodgers game. Gary Cohen, the Mets play-by-play announcer, excitedly describes a double by Pete Alonzo to left field. The ball bounces off the wall and rolls around the warning track as a Met runner scores. The father excitedly shouts out:

"Yea, that's the way to hit it, Pete!"

The father's excitement arouses his son's curiosity.

He quickly leaves the playroom to join his father and shares the experience of watching the game. The father, in a childlike manner, describes and perhaps pretends to swing for a base hit just like Alonzo's swing that he just saw on the television screen. The boy begins to imitate his father, and they both rejoice in the feeling of accomplishment in hitting a ball that scores a run.

Shortly thereafter, the child retreats to his playroom and continues to imitate the swing that his father and himself played out. The next day, the child might run out to his backyard flagging his arms similar to the way his father swung the previous evening. This similar scenario may be repeated many times during the course of the baseball season.

The shared experience between the father and son lays the foundation for the child athlete's awareness and identification of the game of baseball. The stage of Awareness in human development is a necessary precursor to the development of a sustained interest in the game and particularly toward active participation.

2. Creativity

The child's individuation with the game is further propelled by the second stage, referred to as Creativity. Creativity is a mental/imaginative process. The child athlete moves from the role of observer to the task of mentally applying themselves as a player. In this stage, the child actually imagines themselves taking a fielding position or hitting in the batting order. The imagination is individualized and proactive.

In Creativity, the child begins to identify with a player that they idolize. The child dreams and emulates the player's mannerisms and swings. The child sits in his room daydreaming that they could, one day, play in the major leagues with or against their idolized player.

The essence of this stage evolves from the fundamental identification with the game to the act of fusing with the game. These daydreams fuel the child's passion for the game and drive them to work harder to achieve their goals.

3. Experimentation:

In stage three, the child takes the playing field. He begins to join his friends in throwing the ball. He bats and swings. This imaginative process allows the child to personalize their experience with the game and develop their own unique style of play. Moreover, creativity also involves the child athlete identifying with a player that he idolizes. For instance, a young baseball player may idolize Aaron

Judge of the Yankees and emulate his mannerisms and moves. He may practice his swing and throwing style. This identification with an idolized player motivates the child to work harder and strive for excellence in their own play.

A child may miss the ball, but the experience of trying is in itself exhilarating. The child tries to slide into a base. In doing so, he rips his pants or scrapes his knee. In this stage of the child athlete's development, he experiments with the game. This is referred to as the experimental stage.

In this stage, children are encouraged to try new things, take risks, and learn from their mistakes. This is a critical stage in their athletic development because it allows them to develop their skills, build confidence, and find their passion for sports.

During this stage, children may also begin to develop their physical abilities, such as strength, agility, and endurance. They may engage in different types of training, such as weightlifting, running, or stretching, to build their physical capabilities and prepare their bodies for more intense training as they progress in their sport.

As children progress through the experimentation stage, they may begin to specialize in a specific sport or activity. This may involve more focused training and competition, as well as the development of more advanced skills and techniques. With the guidance of coaches and parents, children can continue to develop their athletic abilities and achieve their goals.

He becomes the player he imagined so often in his dreams. He now unleashes his proactive creative impulses. For instance, he kneels in a makeshift ondeck circle awaiting his turn to come to the plate. The batter before him hits a single. Now it's his turn to plant his legs at home plate and try to hit the homerun that he saw his hero accomplish multiple times before him.

On the field, he tries to be the acrobatic fielder, similar to Ozzie Smith, Derek Jeter, and Ken Griffy, Jr.

In the experimental stage, the child will swing awkwardly. He may strike out numerous times. He may miss easy routine ground balls. He may overthrow or underthrow the ball to the first baseman. For the child athlete, the fun is in playing. The freedom of playing independently and creatively ignites his interest. As the ball bounces, the child's passion for the game intensifies. The child athlete is free to be creative, and all of his suppressed fantasies in playing the game suddenly come alive.

4. Mastery:

In the final Mastery stage, the child begins to refine his baseball skills. The mastery stage is characterized by consistency, excellence, and a deep understanding of the sport.

In the mastery stage, the athlete has developed a high level of mastery over their physical and mental abilities. They have developed an enhanced understanding of the technical aspects of their sport, as well as a keen awareness of their own strengths and weaknesses. They are able to perform complex movements and techniques with ease and can make split-second decisions based on their understanding of the game.

In addition to their physical abilities, athletes in the mastery stage have also developed a high level of mental toughness. They are able to stay focused and composed in high-pressure situations and are able to bounce back from setbacks and failures. They have developed a strong work ethic and are committed to continual improvement and growth.

Athletes in the mastery stage may also take on leadership roles on their team or in their sport. They may serve as mentors to younger athletes, sharing their knowledge and experience to help others develop their skills and achieve their goals.

Bryce Harper, who started playing organized baseball at a young age and eventually became a professional player in the Major Leagues, is an example of a child athlete in the mastery stage of baseball.

Harper demonstrated a high level of mastery in his sport, developing advanced skills in hitting, fielding, and throwing. He also showed a deep understanding of the game and became a leader on his team, serving as a mentor to younger players and helping to guide his team to success.

Throughout his career, Harper won numerous awards and accolades for his performance on the field, including the National League Most Valuable Player Award in 2015. His success is a testament to his years of hard work, dedication, and practice, and his ability to achieve a high level of mastery in his sport.

The mastery stage is the culmination of years of hard work, dedication, and practice. It is the stage where athletes can achieve their highest level of success and fulfillment in their sport. While it may be a challenging and demanding stage, it is also a rewarding one, as athletes are able to see the results of their efforts and the impact they can have on their sport and their community.

This stage starts when the child matures into early adolescence, age 12. The child-athlete now has the cognitive abilities along with physical mastery skills to enhance his play in a competitive environment. He has assured himself that he enjoys the sport and wants to compete.

At this point, league play and structure become critical in the child's athletic development. However, overindulgence in a rigid league structure can dispel the interest in playing if the process is not gradually introduced. The child athlete needs to continue the play process as he forges forward to become a competitive baseball athlete. The mastery stage is dynamic. It continuously evolves and modifies to meet the child athlete's individual needs consistent with individual maturity. It is a challenging but rewarding stage, where athletes can achieve their highest level of success and fulfillment in their sport.

CHAPTER 3

CREATIVITY: PLAYING THE DREAM

In this chapter, we'll elaborate on the third stage of the child athlete's development, i.e., Creativity. In this phase, the child applies the dream to a real-life situation.

Creativity is a vital aspect of a child athlete's development, enabling them to explore their imagination, think outside the box, and find innovative solutions to life's challenges. During this phase, the child athlete takes their dreams and applies them to real-life situations, harnessing their creative potential. By being flexible, thinking of new solutions, and experimenting with reality, young athletes foster their creativity, making the process enjoyable and fulfilling.

Creativity is being able to use one's imagination to resolve life problems and experiment with reality by being flexible and thinking of new solutions.

Creativity is fun. Baseball serves as a creative outlet, showcasing the role of creativity in a child athlete's journey.

Understanding Creativity:

Creativity encompasses the ability to employ imagination to resolve problems and embrace novel ideas. For child athletes, creativity plays a pivotal role in their growth, encouraging them to think critically, explore uncharted territories, and overcome obstacles. It allows them to break away from conventional patterns, enabling the emergence of fresh perspectives and unique approaches to the game.

The Sandlot Game: A Canvas for Creativity:

To illustrate the creative process in baseball, let us follow the day of a child athlete playing a sandlot game. The sandlot serves as an open space where children can freely express themselves, experiment with different strategies, and learn through trial and error. The absence of strict rules and organized play encourages young athletes to tap into their creative reservoirs. They can invent new game variations, try unconventional strategies, and adapt to changing circumstances on the fly. This environment allows them to express their creativity and experiment with different approaches to the game.

Imagination Unleashed:

As the child athlete steps onto the sandlot, their imagination ignites. They envision themselves hitting the game-winning home run, making awe-inspiring plays in the field, or pitching a no-hitter. This imaginative projection fuels their passion for the game and provides a platform for creative expression.

Flexibility and Adaptability:

During the sandlot game, flexibility becomes a vital trait for the child athlete. As situations unfold, they need to adapt their approach, make split-second decisions, and adjust their strategies on the fly. The sandlot's informal nature allows them to experiment with various techniques, fostering adaptability and honing their problem-solving skills.

Thinking Outside the Box:

Baseball, like any sport, has established conventions and strategies. However, the sandlot environment encourages child athletes to challenge these norms and devise their own methods.

During the creativity stage, children learn to use their imagination to overcome challenges. They may come up with innovative ways to hit the ball, create unique fielding techniques, or develop creative strategies to outsmart their opponents. By doing so, they enhance their problem-solving skills and learn to think critically and adapt to various situations.

* * *

Perhaps the best approach to discussing the process of baseball as a creative outlet is to simply follow the day of a child athlete playing a sandlot game. It is difficult to dispute the notion that children are creative masters.

"Here's to BASEBALL and the Start of Many Great Endeavors!"

It's 6:45 A.M. on a Saturday morning. Joseph spent the entire week contemplating this day as he walked to school, attended his classes, returned home from the school day, and did his homework.

Finally, the day has arrived. Joseph awakens and immediately looks out of his window. He is excited to see that it is not raining. He observes the sun rising. The face of the sun is so bright and yellow and is shaped perfectly round. Joseph does not think of the sun in the context of his latest astronomy lesson: as a star in the sky that offers us heat and light and which provides plants the source for photosynthesis that generates oxygen for the earth that is consumed for human survival.

Joseph sees the sun only through his baseball eyes. He unleashes his great creative abilities as he begins to freely associate the sight of the sun with baseball.

He pictures stitched seams around the sun's face. He imagines how his hand will grasp around the seams of a baseball as he throws out a runner trying to beat his throw to first base. He imagines how large the ball will look as it is pitched to him. He imagines how his Louisville Slugger 32-ounce bat will smack this ball over the fence for that game-winning home run. He imagines being heralded as a star player in the same manner that his neighbor, Rusty, is admired by other kids for his playing abilities. He looks further into the sky and sees the fading night stars being monopolized by the rising morning sun and all those great players of the past who root for him from the baseball diamond in the heavens that encourage his dream of becoming a big league player.

Joseph quickly jumps out of his bed, dresses into his makeshift baseball uniform, awakens his parents, eats breakfast, and prepares himself for his day. He grabs his baseball mitt and cap, which he finds on his bedroom dresser. On days that he is not playing, the bedroom is his imaginary field, and the dresser is his throwing mate as he often throws a rubber Spalding ball against it, and it reliably returns grounders and line drives back to him.

Joseph is now ready to jump on his bicycle. He places his equipment in the aluminum basket attached to the front of his handlebars. He begins to ride to his nearest neighbor, who is anxiously awaiting his arrival. Together, they ride and knock on doors and awaken neighboring families to meet up with those other child athletes who spent a sleepless night looking forward to playing a game of baseball.

The caravan of bicycles, filled with baseball bats, gloves, and other essential equipment, ride toward Jerry McDonald field, located at Alister Street in Port Aransas, Texas. The field is a poor replica of a professional baseball field. Both the infield and outfield contain a higher proportion of crabgrass and weeds than manicured lawn grass. There are several patches of the outfield that have no grass at all. The base path is composed of hardened cracked clay, covered with small rocks and small patches of overgrown grass. The pitcher's mound is relatively flat and uneven. The running bases are covered with dirt and are hardly visible.

Despite the "as is" condition of the field, Joseph and his friends view McDonald's field as a tropical paradise. As they begin to warm up their arms and arrange their equipment, they, perhaps unknowingly, are the forebearers of a baseball lineage that dates back to the mid-nineteenth century.

In past years, thousands of young players came together, established fields out of abandoned lots in urban communities throughout America, and created a game. Country children made baseball diamonds out of cow pastures. The sandlot experience was a platform for child athletes' self-expression and the birthplace of their passion for baseball. Some of these former sandlotters became Hall of Fame ballplayers, and others pursued different avenues with foreverlasting memories of their sandlot careers. For Joseph and his peers, it is the stage and the chance for their personal dreams to come true.

The teams are ready to be chosen. Joseph, the organizer, selects his arch-baseball rival, Rusty, to be the captain of the opposing team. They flip a coin. If it's heads, Joseph will choose the first player for his team; if tails, it would become Rusty's honor.

The coin is tossed, and it is tails. Rusty, to Joseph's chagrin, selects the prized athlete amongst the motley group of available players. He has the freedom to experiment with his dream and enjoy what the game offers him.

There are no parents to be seen in the bleachers. The child athlete does not suffer from undue anxiety about having to obtain a base hit for his parent. He does not have to feel that his parent is living vicariously through his play. He does not have to observe a parent pleading with the coach to have their son play at the expense of benching another player. He does not have to ride home with his parent and listen to comments about how he can refine his playing skills. In the sandlot game, he is free to selfinitiate, be self-critical, and, most essentially, connect with his peers in a fun-ladened creative activity.

The player's independent identity as a child-athlete is gradually forming as he makes the transition from the imaginative/fantasy stage to the creativity phase. It is the period when the passion for baseball assumes its own life cycle. This is also a critical juncture in the emotional progression of the child-athlete.

But the child-athlete who ultimately succeeds in procuring a professional baseball career may not be the "preferred" player chosen for the sandlot team at this stage in his maturation process. He might have been the third or fourth player chosen for Joseph's or Rusty's team. His maturation to "star player" status is delayed at this time. But similar to his peers, he has an equal opportunity to test his skills and continue experimenting with the game until he is ready to advance to the next level of play.

To divert for a moment, in an academic environment, parents, teachers, and helping professionals pride themselves in understanding that every child matures and learns at an individual pace. The child who becomes a scholar in adulthood may have blossomed academically either in high school or college. The essence of early child development is to offer support, encouragement, and the proper environment to succeed. At some unknown point in time, the child will ultimately determine how he pulls his experiences together.

The child athlete undergoes a comparable maturation process. Athletic maturation can be affected by emotional and physical variables that may delay the child athlete's development. Nevertheless, their growing passion for the game enables them to persevere by continuing to play and indigenously refining their skills. The early sandlot experience offers a patient environment that solicits their creative energies and fosters their gradual individuation as athletes.

The process continues until all the players are grouped together on either Joseph's or Rusty's team. No player is left out or benched. Each plays an integral role on the team.

Even the poorest player acknowledges that he is needed and accepts the fact that he will bat ninth in the order and play right field, where a ball is least likely to be hit during the course of the game. Nevertheless, he is a member of the team and is socially connected to the other children in his neighborhood. The events of this ballgame will be as memorable to him as it is to Joseph, Rusty, and the others who possess greater athletic abilities and perceive this experience as only a stepping stone to fulfilling their dream of becoming a professional baseball player.

The play begins. Within the first few innings, anything and everything has occurred. These sandlot players have experienced how multiple errors can set their team back to a score of 7-2. Some heroes on the winning side learned the beauty of how hitting the ball over the shortstop's head could lead to an inside-thepark home run. The catcher quickly realizes that a ball thrown in the dirt by the pitcher and rolled to the backstop makes it impossible for him to throw out a runner stealing a base.

Despite the inequities of the score at this point, there are no quitters. Every player is using his creativity, consciously or subconsciously, in playing the game. They pretend game strategies. They improvise the batting stance of their favorite big league player. They use their ingenuity trying to hail fly balls in a classic Willie Mays Basket-style catch.

The imperfection of their play is fun and carefree. The spirit of playing is to foster individuality; every player showcases their athletic talents to the best of their abilities. The dream of being the player they wanted to be is finally being expressed on the playing field.

In this game, there are no coaches. The player is left free to play out his own thoughts without adult interference. He does not have to fear that he will be taken out of the game because he made an error or two and struck out more than once. He does not have to worry that he did not properly back up a throw by positioning himself in the appropriate ordinal position on the field. At this point in his young baseball career, he does not have to apply the refined techniques of hitting, assuming he has the cognitive capacity to understand the theory. Cognitive theorists have clearly pointed out that a child's ability to apply abstract concepts begins approximately at the age of twelve. At this point in his socio-cognitive development, he is simply able to face success and failure on his own.

To introduce child-athletes into an organized little league in the preadolescent years may be too premature and counter-productive. Many little league coaches, who volunteer their time and are well intentioned in helping a child, would, understandably, strongly dispute this point of view. The International Little League Foundation, headquartered in Williamsport, Pennsylvania, would protest this argument as well.

A child can join a little league organization as early as the age of five. Coaches attempt to nurture the child athlete in accordance with their age-expected skills and their demonstrated athletic abilities. For instance, a child at the age of 5, plays tee ball, hitting off a stand that holds the baseball stationary.

At age 7, the little leaguer graduates to live pitching. The playtime is rationed and structured. The rationing of play time also becomes apparent. The so-called talented players start to gain more time on the field, and the mediocre player obtains less. The discrepancy in playtime widens even further in the progression of time. The opportunity for self-expression on the field is controlled.

Back at the sandlot field, Joseph and his teammates reduce the deficit of the score in the latter innings of the game. In the eighth inning, the score was 7-6. Joseph's team became more confident and focused. They felt comfortable competing with Rusty and his mates. The intimidation factor, prevalent in the earlier innings by the wide gulf in the score, gradually waned. They were no longer making as many errors. They stood at home plate, determined to hit the ball and move the runners. They were clearly emerging as formidable competitors.

In the ninth inning, the score was still 7-6; in favor of Rusty's team. Joseph's team had a man on first in the bottom of the ninth. Joseph came to the plate with two men out. He found himself in a dream spot. He reflected on the majestic visions he had earlier that day when he saw the sun rising—hitting the ball over the fence for the game-winning home run.

Joseph took strike one. Then ball one. The pitcher, determined to thwart his heroic fantasy, now wound up and threw strike two. Joseph's mind now wandered. He thought of the famous poem of Casey at the Bat, where Casey strikes out in a similar situation. He quickly consoles himself by thinking of the fictitious character, Jake Taylor, in the movie "The Major League." Taylor, in a Babe Ruth-like fashion, calls the shot and hears the sound of the ball off the bat as he hits a home run in the bottom of the ninth to win the game.

Joseph now plants himself in the batter's box and waits for the pitch. The ball is thrown down the middle, and he hits it high in the air toward right centerfield. The dream appears to become true. But the centerfielder, dreaming of making the game saving catch while Joseph entertained his dream, runs deep into the outfield and catches it.

Rusty's team won this particular game, but the players on both sides were the ultimate victors. Each player had the opportunity to dream of a heroic moment. They had the chance to put their fantasies into action. They found a constructive, creative outlet. They exercised their independence, commenced to shape their young individual identities as child athletes, and most of all, had fun with their friends.

Here, it's also important to note how a coach's attitude toward a player and philosophy of coaching can undoubtedly impact the player's motivation and desire to stick with the game. A negative statement from the coach pertaining to a child's poor performance on a given day may forever subvert the child's passion for the game and quickly sabotage his baseball dreams. Some child-athletes' emotional sensitivity to adult authority figures may severely impact their self-esteem due to a negative statement made by an unsupportive coach. The issue of a child's entry into little league play at a pre-teenage period is, therefore, strongly dependent upon the child's psychological readiness to effectively manage stress, structured play, and criticism and sustain a focused mental attitude.

For example, consider a child playing little league baseball who is struggling to keep up with the pace of the game. The coach, frustrated with the child's lack of progress, makes a negative comment about their abilities in front of the entire team. The child feels humiliated and ashamed and starts to doubt his abilities on the field. The coach's unsupportive attitude has damaged the child's self-esteem and made him question his love for the game.

Furthermore, let's examine an 11-year-old baseball player who is eager to play in the local little league travel team. He has been playing in local leagues for several years and is excited to take his game to the next level. However, his parents are concerned that he may not be emotionally ready to handle the pressure of competitive play and scrutiny from demanding coaches. After discussing the matter with the child and observing his emotional readiness, the parents decide to hold off on joining the travel team for another year. This decision allows the child to further develop his emotional resilience and prepares him for the challenges of competitive play.

In conclusion, creativity in sports is not limited to finding new solutions to game-related challenges. It also extends to the child athlete's ability to use their imagination to visualize success and set ambitious goals. By envisioning themselves excelling in their chosen sport, children tap into their creative powers to drive their motivation and dedication. They create a mental image of their desired outcome, and this visualization can serve as a powerful tool in their development as athletes.

Moreover, creativity in the sports context fosters a sense of enjoyment and fun. When children are encouraged to think creatively, they experience a greater sense of autonomy and ownership over their sporting activities. They become active participants in the process, finding joy in exploring new possibilities, experimenting with different techniques, and expressing their unique style.

As adults, it is crucial to support and nurture children's creativity during the development stage. Coaches, parents, and mentors play a vital role in creating an environment that encourages and values creative thinking. They can provide opportunities for children to explore their ideas, experiment with different approaches, and express their imaginations freely.

In order to foster creativity in child athletes, it is important to create a safe and supportive space where they feel comfortable taking risks and making mistakes. Emphasizing the process rather than the outcome helps children develop a growth mindset, allowing them to embrace challenges and learn from failures.

Additionally, providing diverse experiences and exposure to different sports and activities can enhance a child athlete's creativity. Engaging in a variety of sports helps children explore various movement patterns, strategies, and problem-solving techniques.

CHAPTER 4

FROM STREET FREE PLAY TO CYBER PLAY

The emergence of the personal desktop was one of the most significant inventions in human history. Computers simply electrified our culture by shaping how we interact and communicate. We use the computer to research, learn about historical events, see movies, listen to music, network with our friends, and preoccupy ourselves with playing video games, including simulating sports. Along came the Apple iPhone in 2007, and suddenly, without leaving our homes, we could talk, work, shop, and play interactive games on a handheld screen.

The cyber revolution, coupled with public access to the internet, advanced new challenges for children. They suddenly had access to interacting through the World Wide Web. The need to engage with a host of people to play can now be reduced to only playing with selected friends or playing against themselves individually. Thus, the dynamic nature of child plays significantly changed for the present and future.

The cyber revolution is argued to be a great facilitator in the development of a child. A computer is an assistive tool that helps the academically struggling child to access tutorials and programs to help in learning. It offers the gifted child a medium in which to engage challenging problem-solving tasks and test inquisitive ideas. For the physically challenged, it offers means of cognitive exercises and assistive tools to enhance sensory stimulation, motor refinements, and physical conditioning.

Others recognize the importance of the cyber revolution to child development but argue that the trade-off of spontaneous community play is a major flaw. The child's excessive use of the computer is a leading contributor to increasing social isolation.

However, the cyber revolution phenomenon restricts freestyle play. Children may become overly dependent on these tools and lose their ability to explore the world around them in a creative and imaginative way. Let's imagine:

It's a Saturday morning, and Rodney is eager to play baseball. Rodney has limited resources and loves to play. He leaves his house. He walks to his local baseball field in the neighborhood and there are, at best, a few other potential players, but not enough to play a game. Perhaps the die-hard players of these pickup games can only toss the ball to one another and have a brief batting session. These players did not have the ability to play an 18-person 9-inning game and were reduced to a simple practice with only a few kids which may last no more than 2 hours.

Rodney returns home with disappointment and his mother says, "Hey Rodney, did you get a chance to play?"

"No, Mom. Not enough players. Most of my friends wanted to stay in and be on Facebook, Twitter, and some video games on the computer."

Rodney's mother, too, shares the disappointment and frustration that her son's fun day at the park has resulted in having him stay at home for the rest of his Saturday and be alone.

Rodney's local field is one of many throughout the United States that are empty. There are not many empty lots in urban and suburban communities because they are permitted for development. Despite the limited empty lots, one can pass by any neighborhood and observe fields that are ready for play. Strangely, there are no footprints on the infield or in the batter's box, no used balls along the fence, and no sign of a player having run in the outfield. The field is pristinely marking a landmark for the community and a shrine of the pastime where many children once just gathered to play. Perhaps it is now reserved for a league team that uses it on a scheduled day at a specific bracket of time. The sign posted said: "Unauthorized Entry Prohibited!" Symbolically, the field is lonely and isolated just like those inhabitants who are simulating play in their homes.

There are some parents who feel that structured play through neighborhood league teams is protecting their children. They believe that the world is unsafe and it's best to safeguard their sons and daughters from strangers. The message shapes the attitude of the young mind to be mistrustful. Playing with friends requires adult supervision. It reinforces the suspicion that others are out to hurt, and that the community is dangerous.

Once mistrust and fear envelopes the minds of the young ones, they tend to be reluctant in exploring new opportunities and discovering potential talent that could have surfaced if the embedded fear didn't act as a hindrance. For example, if a child is only allowed to play with other children in a supervised setting, they may not learn how to interact with new people in a natural and confident way. This can be particularly problematic when they enter new environments, such as school or work, where they will need to build relationships with unfamiliar people.

Structured play may also limit a child's opportunities to explore and discover their hidden talents and interests. If a child is only exposed to a limited range of activities, such as sports or music lessons, they may never have the chance to discover other areas where they excel. This can be particularly problematic if the child has a talent or interest that does not fit within the confines of the structured play environment.

If a child is passionate about writing, they may not have the opportunity to explore this interest if their parents only enroll them in sports teams and music lessons. This can be particularly frustrating for children who feel like they are not being given the chance to express their true selves.

Furthermore, structured play can also restrict a child's sense of independence and autonomy. If a child is constantly supervised and told what to do, they may not learn how to make their own decisions or take responsibility for their actions. This can be particularly problematic as they grow older and are faced with increasingly complex decisions.

Some parents adopt the hope that their child's athleticism will be discovered by big league scouts and their child would be signed to an elite college athletic program or pro team. Computer software designers promote the notion that if they could quantify performance, it may improve the chances for the Big Ten athletic program. They enlist into a statistical program and now play is measured, and the fun of just playing is detrimental to the individual performance score. I will refer to this concept as "techno-stat play."

Envision:

Joey is involved in organized league play. The coach is determining the batting lineup and Joey is hitting, .275. 15 hits which include 9 singles, 4 doubles, no triples, and 2 home runs. His on-base percentage is .416 and his slugging percentage .365. The coach assigns him to the 3 spot in the batting order because 3 of his hits, including 1 homerun, were off the opposing pitcher. Also, the pitcher is a lefty while Joey bats right, increasing the statistical probability of getting a hit.

Toward the 4th inning, the opposing pitcher is replaced by a right-handed thrower who has often kept Joey hitless in their earlier matchups. The coach now pinch-hits for

Joey based on his historical statistical performance. In sum, Joey batted once, grounded out from short to first, and by the fourth inning, be compelled to sit on the bench for the remainder of the game and perhaps may not play for several more days based on his team's schedule.

Joey returns home and is facing the pressure to improve his statistical performance to be given a chance to play an entire game. If he fails in this effort, his chances of advancing in league play are diminished, and his hopes of procuring a scholarship or some other great reward dwindle.

The illustration of Joey's challenge on the child athlete now begins at pre-adolescent age. Innovative play is suppressed. The objective now is you need to be the best statistically to play, a recipe for a major letdown if the child is unable to meet the challenge. One result is self-deflation and parental disappointment.

The application of cyber-tech play can be applied best in Professional Baseball. This concept was popularized by Billy Beane, the general manager of the Oakland Athletics. He hired a statistician to assist in enlisting players for the team. A criterion used by the statistician was to determine the probability and percentage of a player's ability to get on base. If the player scored high, Mr. Beane offered contracts to those players. The story of Billie Ball was a Hollywood Hit, played by Brad Pitt as Billie Bean in the movie, Moneyball.

But is cyber-stat play beneficial to children's play? The issue is a topic of ongoing debate amongst educators and child therapists. Studies have supported the cognitive benefits of computer-based game applications as it pertains to the child's movement from concrete to abstract thinking during the early adolescent developmental stages (Verenikina et al. 2010). The focus is on problem-solving skills but deemphasizes the effects of social skills. The emphasis on free play is a means of enhancing individual identity in the context of free play with others.

During the period of the heightened COVID-19 pandemic, the comparison of virtual technology and interactive play became evident. It offered a time when children of all ages were faced to learn, interface, and play with virtual technology. The traditional classroom setting was replaced with audiovisual technology - an electronic gathering of students. As in the traditional class, students used ZOOM to complete assignments and have screen exchanges with teachers and friends. This form of social interaction had limitations as opposed to the customary face-to-face classroom experience.

The consequences are substantial. Anecdotal and statistical studies demonstrated a high percentage of children diagnosed with anxiety. One of the most common mental health issues observed among children during COVID-19 has been anxiety. This may be due to a range of factors, including the uncertainty and unpredictability of the pandemic, social isolation and disrupted routines, and the stresses of online learning. For example, children who are accustomed to regular social interaction with friends and classmates may find it difficult to adjust to the limitations of social distancing and virtual communication. This can lead to feelings of loneliness and isolation, which can contribute to anxiety and depression.

Children who are habitually inclined towards physical activity and social interaction may experience a loss of motivation and energy during periods of social distancing and virtual schooling. This gives rise to feelings of sadness and hopelessness, which can be indicative of depression.

These mental health issues have been linked to a range of other negative outcomes, including an increased risk of suicide attempts. Studies have suggested that suicide attempts have increased among children and adolescents during the pandemic, likely due to a range of factors, including increased social isolation, disrupted routines, and financial stress. For instance, children who have lost loved ones or experienced significant financial stress during the pandemic may be at higher risk of suicide attempts, as these factors can contribute to feelings of hopelessness and despair.

Substance abuse is another issue that has been linked to COVID-related mental health issues among children. Studies have suggested that children who are experiencing anxiety or depression may be more likely to engage in substance abuse as a way of coping with their emotions. This can be particularly problematic as substance abuse can lead to a range of negative outcomes, including addiction, health problems, and impaired academic performance.

Finally, family disputes have also been observed to increase during COVID-19, likely due to the increased stress and uncertainty brought about by the pandemic. This can be particularly problematic for children, as family conflicts can contribute to feelings of stress and anxiety, and may also disrupt their daily routines and academic performance. For example, children who are experiencing conflict at home may struggle to concentrate on their schoolwork or may experience disruptions to their sleep patterns, which can negatively impact their academic performance.

The New York Post examined the effects of the COVID mandates as students returned to class in California (8/15/2022) and reported that "when you isolate children away from a seven-hour school day, where there are no sports, no social activities, they have no choice but to turn to their electronics… And there's only darkness there, as they are already vulnerable and going through puberty and susceptible to a lot of group thinking and conformity." The introverted used masks to hide from the world. Another educator/parent stated that his children experienced "hopelessness and despair." Kids started having these long bouts of depression and despair. They could not play baseball or engage in other social activities; their "hopelessness and despair were pretty dramatic."

Socio-emotional development is critically rooted in a child's mastery of their surroundings and evolving maturity. The longitudinal effects of the social effects on children require further research to be ultimately determined. Nonetheless, children need each other for play and social activity to strengthen their identities and negotiate collaboratively with the challenges of society they face and will face in future years.

Baseball, as a team sport, helps to emphasize skills that are essential in the maturation of cognitive, emotional, and physical characteristics. The child athlete, in communication with their peers, can choose sides (dividing the players into teams), negotiate rules, embrace a sense of community, overcome loneliness and isolation as well as feel a great sense of elation that they are expressing their hidden talents. Even the poorest player in the group is accepted in the greater boundaries of the baseball diamond.

Now we face a new challenge as Artificial Intelligence (AI) is adopted to simulate human behavior. Software engineers are inventing robotics for tasks that have been performed by our labor force. But robots are also being designed to act as playing partners in ordinary games, including sports. Someone can compete in a video game against a computer program. In baseball, you can bat against your favorite major league pitcher in an interactive batting simulation program.

Does it replace the social-emotional interaction inherent in human play? AI and other advanced computer applications are tools for assisting growth. They are not humans, and kids are not robots. Each child has their individual style of learning and forming social interplay. We need to be cautious in accepting that AI is not the new norm. Kids gathering on the sandlot or local baseball field is the old-fashioned, down-to-earth welcoming mat. It invites spontaneous teammate interaction that is part of the baseball and emotional-creative experience.

Moreover, traditional forms of play often require children to use their creativity and imagination in order to engage fully in the activity. This can be particularly important for developing skills such as problem-solving, critical thinking, and innovation. In contrast, many AI and computer-based games provide pre-determined scenarios and limited opportunities for creative problem-solving, which can limit a child's ability to develop these important skills.

Traditional forms of play often involve physical activity and the development of gross motor skills. For example, playing a game of soccer or basketball requires children to run, jump, and coordinate their movements in order to be successful. This type of physical activity is essential for developing physical fitness and overall health. As opposed to this, many AI and computer-based games require little to no physical activity, which can contribute to sedentary behavior and the development of health problems such as obesity.

Physical activities provide a sense of connection to the natural world and the community. This type of connection is important for developing a sense of belonging and a sense of place. Many AI and computer-based games are designed to be played indoors and can lead to a sense of disconnection from the natural world and the community.

For parents, the aim is to promote play and avoid social withdrawal and other conditions of social deprivation. AI has its place in our skill development, but it cannot replace traditional methods of play. It is important to recognize that each child has their individual style of learning and forming social interplay. While some children may thrive on the structure and predictability of AI and computer-based games, others may struggle with this type of learning and social interaction. Therefore, it is important to provide a variety of play options and opportunities for children, including traditional forms of play as well as AI and computer-based games.

Encourage children to recognize that spontaneous pick-up play was and needs to be the play of the now and the future. It cannot become a relic of the past. The long-term effects of increasing computer simulation play, and cyber play, can lead to a host of physical and emotional disorders stemming from social isolation. As we continue to integrate technology into our daily lives, it is important to recognize the value of traditional forms of play and to provide children with a variety of play options and opportunities.

Social isolation is a Disease!!!

CHAPTER 5

CAN I BE INCLUDED? THE SPECIAL NEEDS EXPERIENCE

Children with special needs often face challenges when it comes to participating in team sports. These challenges can range from physical and cognitive delays to emotional disorders that make it difficult for them to keep up with their peers.

Such children are often excluded from team sports. Special needs encompass youngsters that have learning difficulties, poor eye-hand coordination, difficulties with fine motor skills, and emotional disorders.

Studies have shown that participation in team sports can have many positive benefits for children with special needs. For example, a study published in the Journal of Autism and Developmental Disorders found that participation in a Special Olympics program had positive effects on both the physical and social development of children with autism spectrum disorders. Another study published in the Journal of Intellectual Disability Research found that children with intellectual disabilities who participated in a sports program had improved physical fitness, selfesteem, and social skills.

Despite these positive findings, children with special needs are often excluded from team sports. One reason for this is that many coaches and programs are not equipped to handle the unique needs of these children. For example, children with physical disabilities may require specialized equipment or modifications to the playing field, while children with cognitive delays may require extra instruction or assistance. Without these accommodations, these children may struggle to keep up with their peers, which can lead to frustration and feelings of inadequacy.

Often these children are not chosen to participate in multiple group activities because their athletic abilities are inferior to the mainstream players. In school programs, they are segregated into small groups of "children like them" while the others enjoy the benefits of a full range of sports activities.

Parents who raised special needs children wonder if their children can participate in the activities of the mainstream world. As a father to a special needs child, I, too, can completely understand this concern.

My son, Jeffrey, always an inspiration to me, was born with autism and pervasive developmental delays. In the early years of his life, he was able to blend with the other children since his disabilities were not obvious. Jeff joined others in playgroups, and no one made fun of him. By age 7, the differences in his intellectual and physical delays became noticeable. The invitations by his age peers ceased. Their parents also stopped inviting Jeff, believing that their kid could do better than playing with him. Any chance of joining an organized baseball team abruptly ended when he ran the bases not to advance from first to second or home, but to run away from the hard-hit ground ball. He was no longer a teammate. The long period of loneliness from being excluded began for years thereafter.

The discussion of special needs in baseball and other sports was historically a sore topic. Over the years, the literature and news on the disabled were of minimal focus. It was until the founding of the Special Olympics in 1960s, by Eunice Kennedy-Shriver, the sister of President John Kennedy. Mrs. Kennedy developed the Special Olympics organization in honor of her disabled sister, Rosemary Kennedy. Mrs. Shriver was a visionary who began her groundbreaking work in the 1950s by devoting herself to the inclusion of special needs children and adults in sports. With the support of President Kennedy in the early 1960s, the organization flourished and had its inaugural competitive event in 1968. This group of athletes became suddenly noticed by the public and media. In time, the mission of Mrs. Kennedy Shriver and others gradually infused our national consciousness.

Later, professional athletes with disabilities gained notoriety. One of the most famous was Jim Abbott, the one-armed pitcher who threw a no-hitter while playing for the New York Yankees. The bias toward disabled athletes slowly waned as their greatness emerged.

Despite these efforts, children with special needs struggled to find acceptance in the community. A great many of these were not seen on the playing fields. The reason is they cannot catch a fly ball consistently, throw a baseball far or swing a bat. They are the easy out.

However, disabled children offer great encouragement to a local team. They can be sitting on the bleachers watching their siblings having fun competing with other players while they are loudly cheering. It is one means of helping them engage in the baseball experience.

They are great fans. They watch their favorite team on television and can recite every statistic and name of every player. This, too, helps them stay peripherally involved in baseball, which is the closest connection to them in actually playing the game.

A typical scene:

The little league team is recruiting for the season. The boys of spring are preparing their gloves, throwing catches in their backyards, and waiting for the call from the coach to learn of their selection on a team.

Travis, a member of last year's all-star team, with extraordinary talent, is obviously one of these first selected. He can throw a bullet from the outfield, run like a deer, and hit the ball a mile.

Mike is one of the players with average ability. He can bat, run and throw reasonably well. Thus, he meets the standard and is given a uniform.

Adam has learning disabilities. He processes information slowly, which takes time to teach him fundamental baseball skills, especially in regard to hitting and throwing. His balance is awkward, impeding his running speed.

Adam, unfortunately, does not make the team. He is told that he can try out next year when his skills improve, or he can help out the team this season by being the bat boy. Adam is out before he made a single play.

However, Adam's dejection from this year's roster extends beyond the league. He attends school, and he is left out of other conversations of last night's matchup between the Bombers and the Eagles. He is not invited to the socials. He may even be called names and bullied by some of the insensitive players that see him as an outcast. They make it clear that Adam cannot be a member of their club. After school, Adam goes to his room. He plays video games and cries silently into his pillow.

The Horizon of Hope:

The inclusion of special needs can be found in Free Style Play. The rigidness of league standards is essentially nonexistent. Adam, along with those with similar abilities as his, has a chance to participate. There are no tryouts, and the expectation to win is overshadowed by the need to simply have fun. The better players are more apt to bypass skill in exchange for having players to compose teams. The less abled player may not play critical positions, such as shortstop or pitch, but can be placed in deep right field and bat last in the lineup. Adam is now playing, and the thrill is greater than enjoying an ice cream sundae on a hot summer afternoon.

There are also many anecdotes along with documented accounts of organized team coaches and players who showed empathy to the special needs who want to be players. The story of Shay by EJ Nolan describes a thrill of a lifetime for a young boy who was dying of cancer and was able to have the one heroic feeling of success.

The Day Shay Got to Play:

Two teams had gathered for a game
At the Playground field that day
The sun was low when I drove up, with
my son whose name is Shay
Now, Shay's a lot like other kids,
and a lot like you and me

But his playing had been limited, by his disability
I thought how much I loved the game
as we saw the field that day
Then Shay looked up and asked me:
"Dad, do you think they'll let me play?
I didn't hold out too much hope.
Thought they'd put up a fight
But one shortstop said, We're down by six, I guess
It'd be all right
The bottom of the eighth began as
evening turned to night
His team got three more runs and then
they sent Shay out to right
He stood there proudly, with his daddy's
glove. A twinkle in his eye,
And a smile that spread from ear to
ear, more brilliant than the sky.
"Three up three down!" the umpire called,
And Shay hadn't made a catch
Three runs behind. Just three more outs,
As Shay's team came to bat.
They loaded up the bases, And Shay stood there on deck.

My heart was in my throat, I thought
"They won't let Shay bat next."
A cold wind blew across that field, and I began to pray.
I looked up and gave a yell, as they tossed the bat to Shay.
Shay's team, in one bold gesture, had given up the win
But then to my surprise, The pitcher
moved a few steps in
He tossed it over under hand, but
poor Shay swung too late
And then the pitcher moved a few steps closer to the plate.
This time he lobbed it really slow
Shay swung and tapped the ball
The pitcher picked it up and heaved
it, Toward the left field wall!
Then from the stands there came a roar
Like fireworks had burst, and all the players on the field
Yelled "Shay, go run to first!
Well Shay had never made it onto first base in his life
The fielder out in left wound up
and threw the ball to right

They knew what his intention was
without uttering a word

The shortstop ran to second, and
pointed Shay toward third

When Shay's foot landed on third base,
His smiling face just shone

And all the players on both teams, were shouting
"Shay run home!"

I knew that no one there that day would ever be the same
When Shay set both feet on home
plate - "The Hero of the Game"

Somewhere angels are laughing

But one dad shed tears that day

For that one Grand Slam - meant *Both* Teams Won...

The Day Shay Got To Play.

*(The Day Shay Got To Play by NJ Nolan -
Printed in Baseball Almanac)*

"The Day Shay Got to Play" serves as a powerful reminder of the importance of providing opportunities for children with disabilities to participate fully in activities like baseball. It highlights the immense benefits of inclusion, not only for the individual but for the entire community. The essence of baseball is beautifully captured as a catalyst for unity, personal growth, and the celebration of the human spirit.

Throughout the poem, Shay's triumphs and challenges on the field are vividly depicted, capturing the range of emotions he experiences. From hitting the ball and running the bases to facing moments of uncertainty and making mistakes, Shay's journey mirrors the universal human experience of growth, resilience, and self-discovery.

The poem also highlights the profound impact Shay's participation has on those around him. The players and spectators witness the joy, determination, and courage that radiate from Shay's every move. They gain a deeper understanding of the power of inclusivity, empathy, and the transformative potential of embracing diversity.

Similar stories are told. One player wrote a very moving account of his "Lessons in Baseball." He begins by saying, "I played baseball whenever and wherever I could. I played organized or sandlot. I played catch with my brother, my father, and with friends. If all else failed, I'd found a rubber ball off the porch stairs imagining all the wonderful things happening to me and my team." Then along came Gordon. "The kindest way of describing Gordon's baseball skills is to say that he did not have any. He couldn't catch. He couldn't hit the throw. He couldn't run. In fact, Gordon was afraid of the ball." Gordon was told by players with the instruction from their coaches: "get lost."

One coach advocated for Gordon. He informed the league that Gordon was fit for his team. The coach gave Gordon extra attention to teach the fundamental skills of baseball. The writer of this moving story of Gordon concludes, "I learned a lot from my coach that summer, but my most important stories weren't about baseball. They were about character and integrity. I learned that everyone has worth, whether they can hit 300 or .030. I learn that we can all have value, whether we can stop the ball or have to turn to chase it. I learned that doing what is right, fair, and honorable is more important than winning or losing." The author of this story was the son of the coach who gave Gordon a chance. Whether the team won or lost the league title that year, they were winners in the decency of life (Moorman).

The stories of Shay and Gordon are demonstrations of empathy. Talented players offered and rallied behind kids with special needs to give them a chance of having a heroic moment and a chance to participate as a team. They strove for the greater good of others instead of achieving personal goals and wins. Most importantly, they found personal and social value in playing with kids of all backgrounds and races, as well as with those who did not have the physical and emotional abilities to play ball naturally. Baseball is more than a game; it's a lesson in acceptance, sharing, facing challenges, winning, and losing as one.

The great promise arrived with the enactment of The Americans with Disabilities Act (ADA) of 1990. The spirit of the law prohibits discrimination against people with disabilities. The disabled were given a chance. The opportunities were legally sanctioned. The nation was put on notice that the disabled are equal members of our mainstream society. Consequently, building structures, educational curriculums, job opportunities, and sports programs were modified to accommodate the disabled population. The sea of hope for the disabled child toward acceptance, that once was on the horizon, came ashore.

Nationwide new opportunities surfaced to accommodate children with special needs. Some with very innovative approaches. For example, The Challenger Little League of The Southern Tier in Vestal, New York, is a baseball league for special needs children ages 6 to 21. The Challenger Division of Little League Baseball provides children with physical and intellectual disabilities the opportunity to play baseball in a supportive and inclusive environment. The program makes accommodations for players with disabilities, such as using a tee instead of pitching to help players with poor eye-hand coordination, and providing a buddy system to assist players who may require extra support. They have an open-door policy with players joining teams at any time during the season. Players with a wide range of disabilities are offered coaching, encouragement, and the ability to be on a team. Adaptive equipment is also used to help the player succeed. This program, like many that are growing throughout the country, is gaining success beyond team wins or losses, but in the mission of inclusion.

In the recent past, a variety of programs and initiatives have been developed to help children with special needs participate in team sports. The Special Olympics provides year-round sports training and athletic competition for children and adults with intellectual disabilities. The program offers a variety of sports, including basketball, soccer, swimming, and track and field, and provides specialized coaching and accommodations to help these athletes succeed.

There are also a variety of local programs and initiatives designed to help children with special needs participate in team sports. For example, some schools offer adapted physical education programs that provide specialized instruction and accommodations to help these children succeed in physical activity. Additionally, some community sports leagues offer inclusive sports programs that are designed to be accessible to children with a variety of abilities and disabilities.

The International Little League Organization in Williamsport, Pennsylvania, also endorsed new programs to promote free play and inclusion. The program is called Sandlot Play. Kids play by their own rules. The pressure of winning and losing is not as critical as having fun. Testimonials from multiple affiliated little league teams, such as in Lake Forest, Illinois, report the enhanced baseball and community skills learned from the experience, one being that all players play.

Still, many barriers impeded the inclusion of the special needs player in sports. But the efforts of alternative sports programs and free play enable these players to **finally stand in the batter's box.**

CHAPTER 6

THE GREAT DIVIDE

At the age of 13, child athletes rethink their commitment to playing sports seriously. This means that their involvement in free play and league participation in Little League may dwindle. Studies indicate that 70% drop out of playing sports.

Multiple reasons may account for this phenomenon:

Biological Changes: Puberty in early adolescence is a period of biological maturation that marks the transition from childhood to being a young adult. This affects behaviors, mood, interests, and priorities. For instance, the surge of hormones during puberty can cause mood swings, making children feel more irritable and emotional, which can affect their motivation to participate in sports. Additionally, children may become more interested in other activities, such as socializing with peers, dating, and pursuing hobbies, which may take away from their time and commitment to sports.

Preference: The individual begins to evaluate their short- and long-term decisions in directing their focus onto other vocational goals. Children's priorities may shift during puberty as they begin to think about their future. They may become more focused on their academic performance, extracurricular activities, and future career goals, which may lead them to prioritize their time differently. For example, they may spend more time studying or preparing for college applications rather than participating in sports.

Natural abilities: Some recognize their lack of baseball talents that begin to separate them from peers with more exceptional athletic skills. Baseball teams have become more competitive. Therefore, team tryouts are more stringent, and coaches are highly selective of those players that make the cuts.

Passion: The child must enjoy what they are doing. If they do not love to play baseball, they will drop out regardless of their athletic talents. Some may pick up other sports interests like swimming, track, and other individually oriented sports.

Burnout: Burnout is a state of physical, emotional, and mental exhaustion caused by prolonged and excessive stress, often resulting from participating in sports without adequate rest or recovery time. The athlete's motivation to keep pace with practice and game schedules becomes burdensome, leading to dropout. There are several factors that can contribute to burnout in young athletes. One of the most significant is the pressure to perform. Children who feel intense pressure to win or meet expectations may feel stressed and overwhelmed, leading to burnout. This can be compounded by overtraining, a lack of rest or recovery time, or insufficient sleep, all of which can contribute to exhaustion and burnout.

Another factor that can contribute to burnout is a lack of enjoyment or fun. If a child is not having fun while participating in sports, they may begin to feel disengaged and lose interest over time. This can be caused by a variety of factors, such as a lack of social connection with teammates or coaches, a lack of autonomy or control over their participation, or a lack of intrinsic motivation to play.

Peer Influence: Friends engage in non-sports activities, and other ways of spending free time start to become more exciting. It's very likely for kids to lose and adopt different interests over time.

At this stage of development, adolescents are striving for autonomy and a sense of identity. They often seek validation and acceptance from their peers, which can lead them to align their interests and activities with those of their friends. If their immediate social circle is moving away from sports, it is natural for children to follow suit in an attempt to fit in and maintain their social connections. The desire for novelty and the opportunity to try new things can be particularly enticing during this developmental stage. Non-sports activities, such as music, art, technology, or social clubs, offer a different set of challenges and opportunities for self-expression. Adolescents may be drawn to these activities as they explore different facets of their identity and discover new passions and talents.

Additionally, the influence of media and popular culture cannot be overlooked. Teenagers are exposed to a wide range of media content, including movies, TV shows, social media, and online platforms, which often highlight and glamorize non-sports activities. These depictions can create a sense of excitement and desirability around alternative hobbies, further fueling the appeal for adolescents who may be seeking something different from sports.

Mental Health: Mental health issues can also be a significant factor in causing children to drop out of sports. The pressure to perform well in sports can exacerbate existing mental health conditions or trigger the onset of new ones, such as depression and anxiety. Children who are struggling with mental health issues may not have the energy or motivation to keep up with demanding practice and game schedules, leading to burnout and eventually dropping out of sports.

Research has shown that there is a strong connection between sports participation and mental health in children. Playing sports can help boost self-esteem, reduce symptoms of anxiety and depression, and provide a sense of community and belonging. However, the pressure to perform well and the fear of failure can also cause mental health issues in children, particularly if they are already struggling with mental health conditions.

Alcohol/Drug Abuse: The increase in drug and alcohol experimentation as well as addiction, interferes with the young mind's judgement, social connections, physical strength, and overall performance. Substance abuse can interfere with judgment, social connections, physical strength, and overall performance, making it difficult for young athletes to excel in sports.

Substance abuse can have a range of negative effects on young athletes. Alcohol and drugs can impair judgment, leading to risky behaviors or poor decision making both on and off the field. Substance abuse can also lead to decreased physical performance and coordination, making it difficult for athletes to perform at their best. Additionally, substance abuse can damage social connections, leading to isolation and a lack of support from teammates, coaches, and family members.

One of the primary reasons for substance abuse among young athletes is the pressure to perform. The pressure to excel can be overwhelming, leading some young athletes to turn to alcohol or drugs as a way to cope with stress or anxiety. This can be compounded by the culture of sports, which may normalize heavy drinking or drug use.

Family: Family finances can limit purchasing of equipment, fees and travel team expenses. Divorce or parental abandonment can create stress and upheaval in a child's life, leading to a lack of motivation or interest in participating in sports. In addition, family financial constraints can limit a child's ability to purchase equipment or pay for fees and travel team expenses, which can hinder their ability to participate fully in sports.

Moreover, family conflicts or issues can lead to negative experiences in sports. Parents who pressure their children to perform or place unreasonable expectations on them can cause anxiety and stress, leading to a lack of interest or burnout. Sibling rivalry or jealousy can also cause tension and conflicts on and off the field, leading to a negative experience for the athlete.

On the other hand, supportive family environments can positively impact the athlete's motivation and interest in sports. Parents who encourage their child's interests, provide emotional support, and attend games and practices can create a positive atmosphere that fosters the athlete's development and growth.

Research has shown that positive family dynamics can have a significant impact on an athlete's success in sports. A study published in the Journal of Youth and Adolescence found that athletes who reported positive parent-athlete relationships had higher levels of sports enjoyment, motivation, and self-esteem. In contrast, athletes who reported negative relationships had lower levels of enjoyment and higher levels of anxiety and stress.

Parental Behavior: The need for a parent to live vicariously through their child can be overwhelming and exceed reasonable expectations of just playing for fun. Parents who have argued with a coach or with other parents in the stands can embarrass or shame the athlete for wanting to play. One of the most common ways parental behavior can hinder a child's interest in sports is when parents have unreasonable expectations or put too much pressure on their child to succeed. Parents who push their child to win at all costs or become star athletes can lead to feelings of anxiety, stress, and burnout in the child. In extreme cases, this pressure can cause a child to lose interest in sports altogether.

Another way parental behavior can hinder a child's interest in sports is when parents live vicariously through their child's accomplishments. Parents who project their own unfulfilled athletic dreams onto their children can lead to feelings of resentment and pressure for the child. This pressure can cause the child to feel as though they are playing sports for their parent's approval rather than their own enjoyment.

Poor Coaching: The young adolescent is highly impressionable and susceptible to the opinions of an authority figure. A coach's assessment or even a negative statement can discourage a young player from wanting to continue being on the team. If a coach is too demanding, harsh, or unresponsive to a player's needs, it can quickly turn the athlete off from sports.

A study published in the Journal of Applied Sport Psychology found that athletes who perceived their coaches as controlling and unsupportive experienced higher levels of burnout, stress, and anxiety. Such athletes were also less likely to enjoy sports, which could lead to a decline in their commitment to playing. In contrast, athletes who had positive relationships with their coaches reported higher levels of intrinsic motivation, enjoyment, and self-esteem.

Poor coaching can also manifest in a coach's lack of attention to individual players' needs and abilities. If a coach does not provide adequate feedback, instruction, or support to a player, it can lead to frustration and a lack of progress. Similarly, if a coach fails to recognize and acknowledge a player's contributions, it can lead to feelings of insignificance and disengagement.

In addition to affecting individual athletes, poor coaching can also impact team dynamics. If a coach shows favoritism or does not address conflicts or issues among players, it can create a toxic environment that discourages teamwork and camaraderie.

It is important to recognize that this shift in interests is a natural part of adolescent development. As children grow and mature, their tastes, preferences, and priorities evolve. While it may be disappointing for parents or coaches to see their child lose interest in sports, it is essential to support their exploration of new activities and respect their choices. This support can help adolescents navigate their evolving identities and find new sources of fulfillment and personal growth.

However, it is also worth noting that this shift away from sports may not be permanent for all adolescents. Some teenagers may rediscover their love for sports later in life or find a way to integrate it with their newfound interests. The key is to maintain open communication, encourage a balanced approach to various activities, and provide opportunities for adolescents to make their own choices while fostering a supportive and accepting environment.

All in all, adolescence hallmarks the great divide between those that continue their athletic pursuits and the majority that phase out. This process is referred to as the acceptance phase. The baseball player has gone through a stage of maturation into a sport and has now consciously embraced the demands expected of him to advance into the higher levels of competition. Coupled with this stage are the rigors of training.

To illustrate:

I spent 2 summers playing baseball at the Little League compound in Williamsport, PA. In the late 1960s and early 70s, the landscape of the site comprised acres of lush green grounds with rolling hills and multiple baseball fields. A training facility and its landmark centerpiece was the Howard J. Lamade Stadium that hosted the annual Little League World Series. For a kid who played on sandlots, on cement, and on the poorly manicured fields of Flushing-Corona Park where home plate was facing Shea Stadium, the home of the New York Mets, the Williamsport experience was breathtaking. It was a thrill for any kid wanting to live the baseball dream.

A day at Williamsport was certainly not a typical Catskill Mountain or Pennsylvania lakefront sleepaway camp. In those camps, kids went swimming in the lake, row boating, hiking, sat around campfires and spooked each other with the stories of CROPSY, the mythical headless horseman that raided the bunks and attacked campers while sleeping.

At Williamsport, the participants were generally in their early to mid-teens. They had extensive baseball experience. Their skills were above average.

The typical day consisted of rising at 6 am, having breakfast, and putting on the practice gear while getting ready for training.

The morning drills, often in hot, humid conditions, consisted of physical workouts, throwing, sprinting, receiving lectures on proper baseball techniques, and practicing gameplay situations with several professional coaches on the field.

By afternoon, you arrived in uniform to play single games and, mostly, double headers until evening. At sunset, players would gather for some social activities, mainly talking baseball. Occasionally, watching baseball on TV. Most memorable for me was the 1970 Major League All-Star Game, where in the 11th inning Pete Rose of the Cincinnati Reds Bulldozed Ray Fosse of the Cleveland Indians at home plate to win the game for the National League. Ultimately, that collision at the home plate ended Fosse's playing career. The thought before returning to my bunk bed: Seeing that hit, do I really want to keep playing?

On Sundays, players had some "free time." But a coach was always available if a player experienced a batting slump or wanted extra fielding drills. The off day became an individualized practice session.

The commitment was clear,

> Talking BASEBALL!
> Eating BASEBALL!
> Practicing BASEBALL!
> Playing BASEBALL!
> Sleeping BASEBALL!

Back in the day and to the present, every August, the Annual Little League World Series is held in Williamsport. The teenage love for baseball is alive and well. For two weeks, Little Leaguers throughout the world gather to compete for the world championship trophy. Many are considered elite players who have gone through a series of playoffs to qualify for this event. They are well coached and are committed to intense practices that elevate their individual skills, which far exceeds the casual player.

However, there is no guarantee that committing to baseball in the acceptance phase leads to Major League play. The challenges are dynamic, and it bottlenecks as one moves up the playing ladder. The division between those that have professional abilities to those that are "just good" widens. At some point in a player's career, one is confronted with the decision to keep either playing or hang up their cleats. Mickey Mantle, the great Yankee slugger and Hall of Famer, often relayed his story when confronted with the decision to play or quit Baseball. As a late teenager, Mantle played in the Yankees Minor League system. Mantle faced a deeply personal conflict manifesting in a playing slump. He was extremely disgruntled with his performance. He thought he did not have what it takes to ultimately play for the New York Yankees. He thought of quitting.

Subsequently, Mantle proceeded to call his father, Charles Mantle, a coal miner from Oklahoma, to take him home. Mickey tells his father that he is homesick and cannot make it in professional Baseball. Charles did not take the call lightly and came to visit his son.

Charles tried to encourage young Mickey about all the years they spent together playing catch, having batting practice, and talking about how baseball led to this opportunity.

The conversation between the father and son was Mickey's Day of Reckoning. Charles told his son to pack up, work at the mines or try to face his mental hurdles and play for the Yankees. Life is never easy. Accept the bumpy road because it isn't fun working in the dark shafts of the zinc mines. Mickey heard the message loud and clear. Luckily for the baseball world, Mantle accepted to face the ensuing challenges to overcome his self-doubts and build his confidence to become one of the greatest players ever.

The exchange between Mickey and his dad is familiar to most parents with adolescents. Kids struggle in their passage from childhood to early adulthood. Parents encourage and support the transition, but often confront teenage ambivalence. For the baseball player at the age of 13 and beyond, the experience ahead is not just fun; it's hard, dedicated, focused work. The athlete must either decide to: Accept it, Commit to it, or Leave it!

CHAPTER 7

OBESITY: NO TIME TO SIT ON THE BENCH

Obesity is a growing adolescent healthcare crisis in the United States. According to the Centers for Disease Control and Prevention (CDC), the prevalence of obesity among adolescents aged 12-19 years increased from 5% in the 1970s to over 20% in the past decade. One of the factors contributing to the rise in obesity among adolescents is the lack of physical activity.

This trend is concerning because obesity is associated with numerous health problems, including type 2 diabetes, high blood pressure, and heart disease. In addition, obesity can have a negative impact on mental health and social well-being. This also suggests that inactivity is a pervasive problem that needs to be addressed to not only reduce obesity among adolescents but also to motivate them to participate in sports activities.

The following could be the contributing factors to this prevalent issue:

Many schools have cut funding for physical education and sports programs, making it harder for kids to participate in organized activities.

Some parents may not have the resources or time to enroll their children in sports or other physical activities outside of school.

It may also be due to changes in kids' interests and preferences for more individualistic activities like video games. A study published in the American Journal of Preventive Medicine found that kids who participated in organized sports had a lower risk of obesity and were more likely to meet the national guidelines for physical activity. The study also found that kids who did not participate in sports were more likely to spend their free time watching TV or playing games on mobile phones or tablets.

The lack of physical activity has become a growing concern. Inactivity can affect the motivation of adolescents to participate in sports activities in various ways. Firstly, a sedentary lifestyle can lead to physical deconditioning, which can make it challenging for adolescents to engage in sports activities. Physical deconditioning is a reduction in physical fitness and muscle strength that occurs as a result of inactivity. This can cause adolescents to experience fatigue and discomfort when engaging in physical activities, leading to a lack of motivation to participate in sports activities.

Secondly, inactivity can lead to social isolation, which can also affect the motivation of adolescents to participate in sports activities. Adolescents who are physically inactive are likely to have limited social interactions, which can cause them to feel disconnected from their peers. This can lead to feelings of loneliness and a lack of motivation to participate in sports activities, which may involve socializing with others.

Thirdly, inactivity can lead to a lack of self-esteem and confidence among adolescents. Lack of physical activity can lead to poor body image and negative self-perceptions, which can make adolescents feel less confident about their physical abilities. This can cause them to feel apprehensive about participating in sports activities, leading to a lack of motivation to engage in such activities.

Many kids are not getting enough exercise, which can lead to obesity and other health problems. A study published in the Journal of the American Medical Association found that only one in four adolescents met the recommended daily physical activity guidelines of at least 60 minutes per day. In addition, the study found that physical activity levels declined with age, with only 18% of 15-year-olds meeting the guidelines.

Let's discuss how parents or guardians can help their children to be more physically and socially active.

Adolescent Nutrition and Fitness:

Nutritional and fitness planning for adolescents is critical for healthy growth and development. According to the Centers for Disease Control and Prevention (CDC), obesity rates in adolescents have tripled over the last three decades, with 1 in 5 adolescents now classified as obese in the United States. Inadequate physical activity and poor nutrition can cause several health issues. Therefore, implementing healthy nutritional and fitness plans during adolescence is crucial for long-term health.

Nutritional Planning:

Adolescents require a balanced diet consisting of carbohydrates, proteins, fats, vitamins, and minerals. A balanced diet can help adolescents maintain a healthy weight, improve their cognitive function, and reduce the risk of chronic diseases. In planning a nutritional diet, one ought to consult with a medical specialist, including a dietician and/or nutritionist, to customize a plan that best meets your specific health needs.

Some key points to consider in planning a diet program for the adolescent is as follows:

Fruits and vegetables: These provide essential vitamins, minerals, and fiber that support brain health and overall well-being. Aim for a variety of colorful fruits and vegetables, including leafy greens, berries, citrus fruits, and sweet potatoes.

Whole grains: Whole grains such as brown rice, quinoa, and whole wheat bread provide important nutrients and fiber that support brain function and overall health.

Lean protein: Protein is essential for growth and development, and can also help to regulate mood and energy levels. Good sources of lean protein include chicken, turkey, fish, eggs, and legumes such as beans and lentils.

Healthy fats: Omega-3 fatty acids are important for brain health and can be found in fatty fish such as salmon, as well as in nuts and seeds such as flaxseed and chia seeds.

Avocado, olive oil, and nuts are also sources of healthy fats that support brain function.

Water: Staying hydrated is essential for brain function and overall health. Encourage children to drink plenty of water throughout the day and limit sugary beverages.

In addition to promoting healthy eating habits, it is important to limit processed and sugary foods, as well as foods high in saturated and trans fats. These types of foods can negatively impact mood, energy levels, and overall health. Encouraging regular physical activity and ensuring adequate sleep can also support children's mental and physical health.

Fitness Planning:

Regular physical activity is crucial for adolescent health. The CDC recommends that adolescents engage in at least 60 minutes of moderate-to-vigorous physical activity per day. Fitness planning for adolescents should include the following:

Cardiovascular exercise: Cardiovascular exercise, such as running, cycling, or swimming, can help improve cardiovascular health, increase endurance, and reduce the risk of chronic diseases.

Strength training: Strength training, such as weightlifting or bodyweight exercises, can help build muscle strength. Weightlifting exercises typically involve the use of free weights, such as dumbbells or barbells, while bodyweight exercises use the weight of the body to provide resistance. Resistance band exercises involve the use of elastic bands to provide resistance.

When designing a strength training program for adolescents, it is important to ensure that it is age appropriate, safe, and effective. Adolescents should start with light weights or resistance bands and gradually increase their weight or resistance as their strength and fitness levels improve. They should also focus on proper form and technique to reduce the risk of injury.

In addition to cardiovascular exercise and strength training, flexibility and balance exercises should also be included in fitness planning for adolescents. These exercises can help to improve the range of motion, prevent injury, and enhance overall physical performance. Examples of flexibility exercises include stretching and yoga, while balance exercises can include standing on one leg or using a balance board.

It is important to note that fitness planning should be tailored to each individual adolescent's needs and abilities. Adolescents should consult with a healthcare professional or certified fitness trainer to determine the most appropriate and effective fitness plan for their goals and physical condition. By engaging in regular physical activity that includes cardiovascular exercise, strength training, flexibility, and balance exercises, adolescents can improve their overall health, well-being, and quality of life.

How Schools Can Play Their Part to Eliminate Obesity Among Teenagers and Kids

One of the most effective ways that schools can help reduce obesity in kids is by promoting healthy eating habits. This can be achieved through various means, such as serving nutritious meals, offering healthy snacks, and educating students on the importance of making healthy food choices. According to a study published in the Journal of the Academy of Nutrition and Dietetics, children who participated in the National School Lunch Program (NSLP) consumed more fruits, vegetables, and whole grains than those who did not participate. Additionally, the study found that the NSLP was associated with lower rates of obesity among students.

Warning of Illicit Use of Diabetic Medications

There has been a recent trend amongst youth to use Ozempic, an injectable medication, for weight loss. There are emerging reports that adolescents and young adults are gathering at "Ozempic parties to show off how the drug has reduced their weight." Ozempic is a serious medication used to treat Type 2 diabetes. Its objective is to regulate blood sugar in adults. This injectable drug is aimed at treating adults and not children. Ozempic use needs to be medically supervised.

The manufacturer of Ozempic, Novo Nordisk, warns that the drug's effects on children under the age of 18 are unknown.

The side effects include inflammation of the pancreas, vision modifications, low blood sugar, kidney dysfunctions, and gastrointestinal distress. Most commonly identified side effects are nausea, vomiting, diarrhea, constipation, and stomach pain.

Mounjaro, produced by Eli Lilly, is similar to Ozempic. It is an injectable drug that is prescribed to adults by certified medical specialists to treat Diabetes 2. It has been studied to benefit some patients who are dually diagnosed with Type 2 diabetes and Obesity.

The use of the Mounjaro drug is regularly monitored through ongoing assessments and blood tests. (Refer to Elli Lilly's website on Munjaro for more information).

The use of diabetes medication is not a fad or a substance to be taken superficially. Its effects are potent and medical oversight is required. The use of amphetamine drugs and high-energy booster drinks may be addictive and counter-productive in achieving the goals of reducing weight, especially obesity.

In addition to promoting healthy eating habits, schools can also encourage physical activity through various means. This can include offering physical education classes, organizing sports teams and afterschool activities, and providing opportunities for students to be active during recess and other breaks throughout the day. According to the CDC, children and adolescents should engage in at least 60 minutes of moderate to vigorous physical activity each day to maintain good health. Research has shown that physical activity is associated with a lower risk of obesity, as well as improved mental health and academic performance.

Another important factor that schools can address to counter obesity in kids is mental peace. Schools can provide a supportive and nurturing environment that promotes mental well-being, and they can also offer resources such as counseling and mental health services to students who need them. According to the American Psychological Association, stress can lead to overeating and weight gain, so it is important to address mental health concerns in order to reduce the risk of obesity.

Finally, schools must also address the issue of bullying, which can have a significant impact on a child's physical and mental health. According to a study published in the journal Pediatrics, children who are bullied are more likely to be overweight or obese than those who are not bullied. This may be due to the fact that bullying can lead to stress, anxiety, and depression, which in turn can lead to overeating and weight gain. By creating a safe and inclusive environment that promotes kindness and respect, schools can help reduce the risk of obesity and other health problems associated with bullying.

I believe that schools in America can really play a critical role in reducing obesity in kids by promoting healthy eating habits, encouraging physical activity, addressing mental health concerns, and addressing bullying. By implementing evidence-based programs and policies, schools can help create a culture of health and well-being that benefits all students. According to a report published by the Robert Wood Johnson Foundation, schools that prioritize health and wellness have been shown to improve academic performance, attendance rates, and graduation rates. As such, investing in the health of our students can have far-reaching benefits for both individuals and society as a whole.

How Parents Can Ensure Good Physical Health of Their Child

While schools and other institutions can play a role in promoting healthy lifestyles and reducing the risk of obesity in children, parents also have an important role to play in ensuring that their kids maintain a healthy weight.

Apart from promoting good nutritional foods, and physical activities, here are some strategies parents can use to assist their kids to be healthy and fit.

1. Limit your child's screen time

Excessive screen usage can result in weight gain and other health issues and is a primary cause of sedentary behavior. By establishing limits and implementing regulations about the use of gadgets like TVs, laptops, tablets, and cell phones, parents can reduce their children's screen time. The American Academy of Pediatrics advises against allowing children under the age of two to spend more than one hour a day in front of a screen.

2. Model Healthy Behaviors

Children's attitudes and behaviors towards food, physical activity, and general health are greatly influenced by their parents. Parents can assist their children in developing lifelong healthy habits by setting a good example for them. This includes prioritizing self-care and mental health, eating wholesome foods, and staying active. 3. Promote a healthy body image

Children who have disordered eating patterns and poor mental health outcomes may be affected by negative body image and weight stigma. By refraining from making disparaging remarks about their children's bodies, stressing the value of health and well-being over appearance, and setting an example of self-acceptance and self-love, parents may help their children develop a healthy body image.

According to research, parental encouragement and participation are essential for preventing childhood obesity. A study that was published in the Journal of the Academy of Nutrition and Dietetics found that parents who are interested in their kids' eating and exercise habits are more likely to have kids who eat well and exercise frequently.

Additionally, a study that was published in the Journal of Pediatrics discovered that parents who prioritize healthy food and exercise in their own lives are more likely to produce kids who do the same. This indicates that parents can have a significant impact on their kids' attitudes and behaviors around food and exercise.

Children who are significantly overweight are more likely to develop a variety of health issues, including type 2 diabetes, high blood pressure, asthma, and sleep apnea, according to the CDC. Obesity can harm a child's mental health and well-being in addition to their physical health, resulting in low self-esteem, social isolation, and despair.

A major public health concern is preventing childhood obesity, and parents are essential to this effort by encouraging physical activity, limiting screen time, supporting healthy food, and modeling these behaviors.

It's important to note here that teaching children good healthy habits from a young age is important because these habits can have a profound impact on their long-term health and well-being. Research has shown that children who develop healthy habits early in life are more likely to maintain these habits as they grow older, leading to a lower risk of chronic diseases and other health problems.

Children's behavior and academic performance can both benefit from healthy habits. Children who regularly exercise had greater cognitive function and academic achievement, as well as better classroom behavior and attendance, according to a report from the Centers for Disease Control and Prevention (CDC). Additionally, a study indicated that kids who eat a healthy meal outperform kids who skip breakfast or eat a poor breakfast in terms of academic performance. The study was published in the Journal of Nutrition Education and Behavior.

CHAPTER 8

AVOID THE BASEPATH OF SLIDING INTO ALCOHOL AND DRUGS

Adolescents need activity, and baseball needs players. Multiple studies examining sports participation among teenagers have shown that as a child reaches the age of 13, there is a significant decline in interest in baseball. As previously mentioned, the average dropout rate is approximately 70%-75%.

The impact of this decision on the child athlete can have significant physical, social, and psychological ramifications. In general, sports represent a means of channeling emotions into a constructive activity that may otherwise be directed into destructive behaviors against self or others.

Furthermore, sports feature a forum for kids to be creative and have fun. Through sports, they learn organizational skills that foster responsible community interaction and later day successful vocational performance.

Let's face reality! Many children are in a state of crisis. There is a growing trend of maladaptive social behaviors, including crime, and a significant increase in alcohol/drug abuse. The National Center for Drug Abuse Statistics found that 1 in 8 teenagers in the United States abused an illicit drug in the year 2020.

From 2016-2020, drug use amongst 8th graders rose by 61%.

A total of 407,000 teenagers aged 12 to 17 were diagnosed with alcohol abuse, while 788,000 met the diagnostic criteria for illicit drug abuse disorder.

YOUTH ALCOHOL ABUSE

In the United States, alcohol is the most commonly abused substance among teens and young adults. A particularly problematic pattern of alcohol consumption among young people is binge drinking, which is defined as consuming a significant amount of alcohol in a brief period of time. A variety of harmful outcomes, such as alcohol poisoning, accidents, and unsafe sexual behavior can result from binge drinking.

1.19 million 12- to 17-year-olds and 11.72 million 18- to 25-year-olds reported binge drinking in the previous month, according to the National Survey on Drug Use and Health.

The statistics below are alarming and substantiate the prevalence of alcohol abuse among today's youth population.

- 25.6% of 8th graders have abused alcohol at least once
- 61.5% of teens have abused alcohol by 12th grade
- 9.15% of all 12- to 17-year-olds used alcohol in the last month
- 2.7% of 12th graders drink daily
- 16.8% of 12th graders have 5+ drinks in a row when consuming alcohol
- 0.4% of 8th graders drink daily; by 10th grade, 1.0% drink daily
- 407,000 teenagers aged 12- to 17-years-old met the criteria for Alcohol Use Disorder (AUD) in the last year

According to research, drinking alcohol during adolescence and the early years of adulthood might affect how the brain develops as well as one's general health. According to a research in the journal Alcoholism: Clinical and Experimental Research, teens who drink heavily can have changes in their brain's biochemical activity and cognitive functioning. Alcohol use throughout adolescence may raise the likelihood of evolving into alcohol dependency as alcohol consumption progresses.

According to another study published in the Journal of Pediatrics, alcohol usage among young individuals has far-reaching harmful effects that go beyond the individual. Accidents involving alcohol are the main cause of death for teenagers and young adults. The National Institute on Alcohol Abuse and Alcoholism reports that 28% of all traffic-related fatalities among teenagers and young adults are alcohol-related.

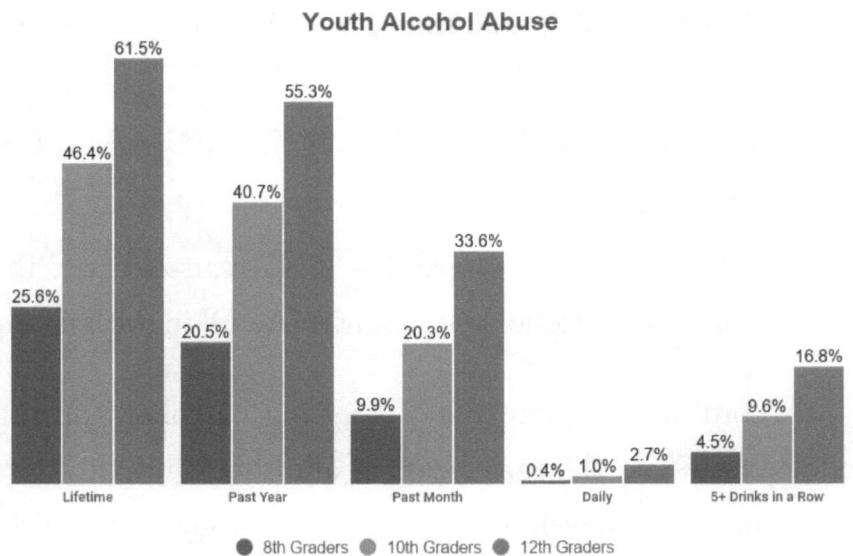

Teenage drug abuse is a significant problem in the United States of America. There have been educational and therapeutic interventions aimed to mitigate the problem, but often new drugs are created to entice greater use. As the population of kids continue to abuse drugs, their academic, social, physical, and mental health will be significantly impacted.

The extent of youth drug abuse is well documented by a series of public health studies.

According to the National Survey on Drug Use and Health (NSDUH), 12.78% of all 12- to 17-year-olds reported using marijuana in the last year. The use of other illicit drugs, such as heroin, cocaine, and methamphetamine, also remains a significant problem among young people.

The NSDUH also reports the following:

- 0.42% of all 12- to 17-year-olds report using cocaine in the last year
- 0.17% report using methamphetamines
- 0.02% used heroin
- 2.52% report misusing pain relievers

The NSDUH also found that the misuse of prescription drugs is increasing among youth, with an estimated 2.1 million adolescents aged 12-17 misusing prescription drugs in 2020. The issue is not limited to one particular demographic, but it affects young people from all backgrounds and social classes.

The situation is quite grave, and drug misuse can have disastrous repercussions. Damage to important organs, including the liver, kidneys, and lungs, as well as an increased risk of heart disease and stroke, are among the physical impacts of drug misuse. Drug usage is frequently linked to mental health problems such as depression, anxiety, and suicidal thoughts. Adolescents who take drugs are also more likely to have future scholastic issues, engage in criminal activity, and struggle to find and maintain jobs.

Drug usage amongst kids affects their judgements which can lead to high-risk behaviors, including unsafe sexual intercourse leading to adolescent pregnancies and sexually transmitted diseases.

Additionally, drug-using adolescents are more prone to commit crimes, drop out of school, and have financial problems. Young people may have few options for rehabilitation due to the prohibitively high expense of drug addiction therapy. Treatment resources for this are limited. There are less than 15,000 treatment facilities in the United States, serving approximately 4 million people of various age groups. Publicly funded outpatient and inpatient treatment programs are overcrowded and are unable to accommodate the demands of patients seeking help. Similarly, private alcohol/substance abuse treatment facilities are expensive and often have waiting lists for admitting new patients.

According to the Substance Abuse and Mental Health Services Administration (SAMHSA), 788,000 teenagers aged 12- to 17-year-olds met the criteria for Illicit Drug Use Disorder (IDUD). Illicit drug use disorder is a serious problem that can have significant consequences for the physical and mental health of young people. It is a condition that is characterized by a compulsive drug-seeking behavior, despite the negative consequences that result. The fact that nearly 800,000 teenagers meet the criteria for this disorder highlights the need for urgent action to address the problem.

This age group is nearly twice as likely to suffer from IDUD than they are to meet the criteria for AUD. Additionally, a significant percentage of high school seniors have abused tranquilizers, hallucinogens, and LSD, further highlighting the extent of the problem.

SAMHSA specifically cites that:

- 7.0% of 12th graders have abused tranquilizers
- 7-5% have abused hallucinogens
- 5-9% have used LSD

OPIOID ABUSE

In the US, the misuse of opioids has risen to the point of a national public health emergency. Opioids are a group of drugs that includes both legal and illicit substances like heroin, as well as prescription painkillers like oxycodone, hydrocodone, and fentanyl. Opioids are extremely addictive and have a number of detrimental effects on health, including overdose and death.

The rise in young people's deaths from opioid overdoses is one of the most alarming trends in opiate misuse. The CDC reports that since 1999, the number of opioid-related deaths among people aged 15 to 24 has grown by 500%. This age group experienced an annual increase in opioid-related overdose mortality of up to 30.7% in the twenty-first century.

The increase in opioid-related mortality among young people is especially concerning since it leads to the loss of human potential and places a heavy financial burden on society. Due to lost productivity, increased criminal justice expenditures, and healthcare costs, the opioid crisis has cost the US billions of dollars. Opioid deaths due to opioids have increased 500% among 15-24-year-old since 1999.

In the 21st century, opioid-related OD deaths among this age group increased by as much as 30.7% annually. There are a number of factors that have contributed to the rise in opioid abuse among young people. One of the main drivers has been the overprescription of opioids for pain management. In the late 1990s and early 2000s, pharmaceutical companies heavily marketed prescription opioids as safe and effective for managing pain. This led to a significant increase in the number of opioids prescribed, which in turn contributed to the rise in opioid abuse and overdose deaths.

High school students who legitimately use prescription opioids are 33% more likely to misuse opioids after high school. Take a look at the statistics below:

- 5.3% of 12th graders have abused opioids other than heroin at least once
- 0.4% of 12th graders have abused heroin

- In the past year, 2.4% of 12th graders abused Oxycontin, while 1.2% abused Vicodin

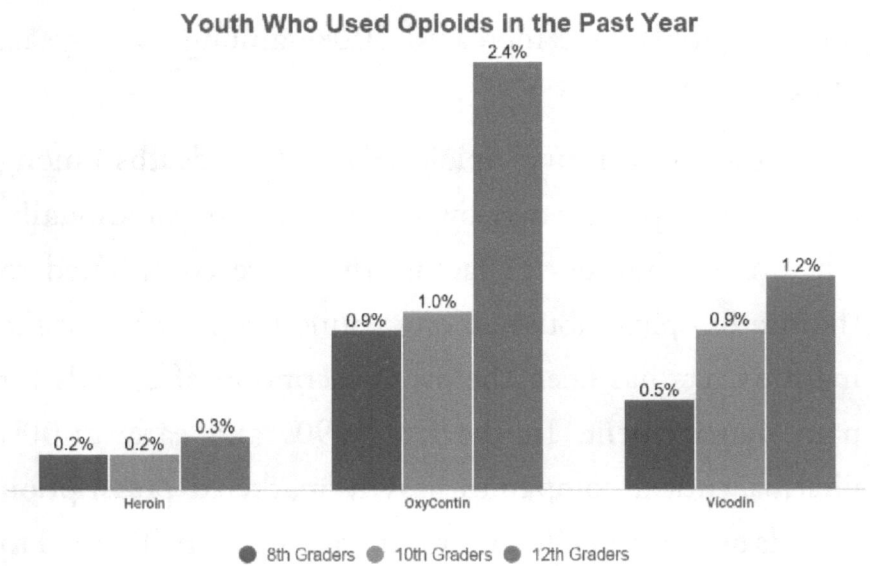

DRUG OVERDOSE DEATHS

The effects of the rise in drug overdose deaths among adolescents are devastating. The loss of young lives is tragic and has far-reaching consequences for families, friends, and communities. The increase in overdose deaths also puts a strain on healthcare systems and resources, which are already stretched thin due to the pandemic.

Drug Overdose Deaths in 10-19 years old as reported by the Center for Disease Control and Prevention **(CDC)** Report by Tanz, LJ, et al., dated December 16, 2022:

From 2019-2021, there was an increase in overdose deaths for adolescents aged 14-18. 94% from 20192020 and 20% from 2020-2021.

The median monthly overdose deaths increased by 109% between July-December 2019 and July-December 2021.

Deaths involving fentanyl (IMFs) increased 182%, as the median monthly overdose percentage from July-December 2019 to the latter 6 months of 2021. Fentanyl, a synthetic opioid that is up to 50-100 times more potent than morphine, is used illegally as a recreational drug and is often mixed with other substances like heroin or cocaine. The increase in overdose deaths involving fentanyl is particularly concerning because of its potency. Even a small quantity of fentanyl can be deadly, and users may not even know they are taking it. In addition, illicitly manufactured fentanyl (IMFs) is becoming more prevalent, which means that it may be even more dangerous as it is not regulated and often mixed with other harmful substances.

It is important to note that the rise in overdose deaths involving fentanyl is not just affecting adolescents.

Fentanyl has been identified as a contributing factor to the overall increase in overdose deaths in the United States in recent years. However, the increase in overdose deaths among adolescents is still alarming and highlights the need for prevention and intervention efforts aimed at this age group.

Contributing variables related to the rise of overdose deaths were expanded access to IMFs, other opiates and bootleg drugs through social media and other avenues of distribution. Overdosing from substance abuse can be accidental and unintentional. The adolescent is unaware, generally oblivious to the toxicity of a drug and its fatal consequences. Peer pressure and experimental curiosity may play a significant factor in the decision to use and accidentally overdose on lethal drugs. Prevention efforts for such drugs can include education and awareness campaigns about their harmful effects, as well as increasing access to evidence-based substance use disorder treatment for adolescents. There may be a need for increased regulation and oversight of the illicit drug market to reduce the availability of dangerous substances like fentanyl.

Cognitively, the adolescent's "pre-frontal cortex, the brain's executive control center, does not fully develop until the mid-20s." (Cohen, 2022).

Drugs and the Surge in Suicide Rates

Suicide has characteristics of intentionality. The individual aims to end their life due to long-standing feelings of depression, hopelessness, a sense of failure, lack of social acceptance, loss of a significant person, rejection by a loved one, and inability to cope with the stressors of daily life. For adolescents, bullying at school and on social media has contributed to a child's desire to terminate his or her life.

The rise in suicide rates, along with suicidal ideations and attempted suicide for teenagers, is alarming. The **CDC** reports that suicide is the second leading cause of death amongst those individuals ranging from ages 15 to 24. This represents nearly 20% of the entire population for that age group. In the past decade, the suicide rate among teenagers rose close to 60%. The pandemic contributed to the uptick of the problem, but the increase preceded the major COVID outbreak in the year 2020.

Below are some lifesaving helplines to follow in case of emergencies:

1. If you are aware of anyone who has made a suicide attempt, call 911 for immediate emergency care.
2. If anyone suggests suicide or has suicidal thoughts, call 911 for emergency medical attention.

3. Anyone in despair and needing immediate professional advice and support, call 988, the National Suicide and Crisis Hotline.

The COVID-19 pandemic also contributed to the rise in drug overdose deaths among adolescents. The pandemic caused significant disruption to our daily lives, leading to increased stress, isolation, and uncertainty. For many adolescents, the pandemic has been a traumatic experience, leading them to seek relief through drug use.

How to Tackle the Problem of Drug Overuse among Adolescents?

The rise in drug overdose deaths has a significant impact on society as a whole. It affects the economy, as it results in lost productivity and increased healthcare costs. It also undermines the social fabric of communities, as it leads to increased crime, homelessness, and other social problems.

To address the rise in drug overdose deaths among adolescents, we need to take a multi-faceted approach. We need to increase awareness and education about the dangers of drug use, particularly among adolescents. We also need to improve access to mental health, substance abuse treatment, and prevention services to avert the rise of drug use and addiction.

Another critical strategy is to reduce the availability of opioids and other highly addictive drugs. This includes implementing stricter regulations on the prescription and distribution of opioids, as well as increasing enforcement against illegal drug trafficking.

We also need to promote alternative pain management strategies, such as physical and occupational therapy and the use of non-addictive medications.

Furthermore, we need to provide support and resources for adolescents who are struggling with addiction. This includes access to evidence-based treatments, such as behavioral therapy and medication-assisted treatment. We also need to ensure that adolescents have access to supportive services, such as housing, employment, and education, to help them overcome addiction and rebuild their lives.

To address this trend, we need to take a comprehensive approach that includes increasing awareness and education, improving access to mental health services, reducing the availability of opioids, and providing support and resources for adolescents struggling with addiction. By working together and promoting healthier, more resilient communities, further loss of life can be prevented.

Treatment Program Models

There is a dire need to establish a greater number of treatment programs that can serve millions of people of all ages suffering from alcohol and drug addiction. Currently, there is a scarcity of services available. Programs are comprised of 3 distinct treatment models: inpatient rehabilitation, intensive outpatient treatment, and psycho-educational programs. The nature of the treatments is described as follows:

In-patient Treatment:

Patients are admitted into a facility and are treated in-house for 28 days. Patients receive group therapy, individual counseling and are engaged in self-help meetings such as Alcoholics Anonymous and Narcotics Anonymous. Family members are also engaged to enhance their understanding and insight if the disease of addiction.

Some facilities may offer detoxification treatment at the outset of the admission to stabilize symptoms that may place the patient at risk when withdrawing from alcohol and/or opiates.

Intensive Medically – Supervised Outpatient Treatment:

This model emerged in the 1980s. It offered alcohol and drug users a community-based rehabilitation program. It was designed for working individuals and as a first step toward rehabilitative treatment prior to determining the need for inpatient care.

The medically supervised program requires physician oversight to determine a patient's treatment plan. The patient is seen by addiction counselors in group and individual therapy multiple times a week for generally 3 treatment hours per visit. After the initial course of treatment, the patient is reduced to fewer days per week. The object of outpatient treatment is to enable the patient to work or attend school and maintain a routine family life as they seek to abstain from their drug of choice.

Psycho-educational Counseling:

This level of intervention provides information and education about the disease of Alcohol and Drug addiction. Lectures, films, speakers, and other training tools are used to enhance learning objectives. These courses are led by teachers, counselors, clergy, police officers, or recovering addicts. This model is not considered medically oriented treatment, though much of the information in these psychoeducational training milieus is utilized in treatment programs.

Treatment Communities:

In this model, patients reside and are offered treatment services in small residential settings for extended periods of time, such as 1-2 years. Patients live away from their families. The patients are expected to participate collaboratively in various community chores in a sober living environment.

Sober Houses:

This model offers an alcoholic or addict a home in the community to reside with others who are attempting to stay sober. This is not considered a treatment setting. However, residents in sober homes are expected to attend treatment programs.

Individual / Group Counseling in a Private Practice Setting:

Patients are assigned a licensed therapist who specializes in addiction treatment and engage with them in either one-on-one, or in group counseling. The patient is generally seen 1-2 times/per week.

Self-Help Groups:

Alcoholic Anonymous (AA) or Narcotics Anonymous (NA). These are meetings held in various settings in the community. Meetings are administered by recovering individuals who offer support and sponsorship for those aiming to lead a sober life.

Given the number of treatment models, there are an insufficient number of services available for the growing population of youths and others suffering from addictions.

To eradicate IDUD, what are the possible preventive measures?

The use of tranquilizers, hallucinogens, and LSD among high school seniors is also concerning. These substances can have a significant impact on the developing brain and can lead to a range of negative consequences. The fact that a significant percentage of high school seniors have abused these substances highlights the need for more comprehensive education and prevention efforts.

Preventing teenage drug abuse requires a multifaceted approach that involves education, prevention, and treatment. Education efforts should focus on providing young people with accurate information about the risks associated with drug use. This education should be delivered in a way that is engaging and relevant to young people, using peer-led programs and social media to reach this population.

Prevention efforts should focus on promoting healthy behaviors and providing young people with alternatives to drug use. This includes promoting physical activity, healthy eating, and social engagement. Community-based programs and afterschool activities can also be effective in providing young people with positive alternatives to drug use.

Treatment options should be made more accessible to young people who are struggling with addiction. This includes counseling, medication-assisted treatment, and peer support groups. These options should be available in a range of settings, including schools, community centers, and healthcare facilities.

CHAPTER 9

STAY IN THE BATTER'S BOX

Multiple studies cite that the dropout rate from baseball and other sports begins at about age 12. As mentioned previously, approximately 70-75% of young adolescents lose interest in playing organized sports. This statistic is very concerning given the harsh realities of studies related to the rise of alcohol and substance abuse in addition to increasing symptoms of emotional disorders.

Parents, coaches, child therapists, and researchers need to find ways to make the sports experience inspirational and compelling. Sports isn't just a healthy physical activity but a coping mechanism. Kids should not be encouraged to phase out of sports given the value of interactive activities.

To examine the issue further, I conducted a survey to understand why the dropout rate was high. The survey comprised a series of questions that addressed how the child athlete became involved in sports; whether the parents encouraged them, or whether they became a reason for them to choose to continue or discontinue playing baseball.

- A total of 141 Middle School respondents completed the questionnaire. Of the 141, 40 were completed by eleven-year-olds, 46 twelve year-olds, and 55 thirteen-year-olds. The response was enlightening.
- The eleven-year-old group demonstrated that 43% played organized baseball and 56% no longer played.
- By age twelve, the group that played organized baseball dropped to 30.5%, and 69.5% were not playing baseball.
- At age thirteen, the number of players decreased to 16% and 83% were no longer involved.

The results highlight and support other studies, as well as observations that adolescent involvement in organized baseball drops significantly over a 3-year period.

Interestingly, the findings of this study found that interest in sandlot baseball and non-structured play was relatively high.

Seventy percent of the 11-year-old respondents indicated that they enjoyed and would participate in playing with friends and family in an unorganized fashion. Some of the respondents may include those in organized sports who would participate with less serious players for the sake of simply playing the sport.

By age twelve, playing sandlot baseball declined to 58% of the respondents, while 41% responded that they would not play organized or free-style sandlot baseball.

However, by age thirteen, the number of players interested in sandlot baseball spiked to 80%, while 20% preferred not to play baseball.

The questionnaire I used for my survey is shared below:

ADOLESCENT QUESTIONNAIRE:

First Name Only:

Age:

1. Do you play baseball?
2. Do you play on a Little League Team?

3. Do you play Sandlot or on a pickup team where you just play with friends for fun?

4. Do you look forward to practice and games?

5. How do your parents feel about baseball?

6. Do your parents push you to go to practice and/or games? Or do you remind them that you have a practice or a game?

7. Do you want to play baseball beyond Little League, such as in High School or College?

8. Do you ever dream of playing Major League Baseball?

9. Do you play on a team with the hope of getting a college scholarship or a professional baseball contract?

10. Do your parents want you to play on a team so you can get a college scholarship or professional baseball contract?

11. In general, do you prefer to play on an organized team or just play sandlot (pick up) baseball?

12. Why do you no longer play baseball?

Total Subjects in Survey = 141

Age 11: 40 Respondents.

- Playing in Little League: 23 subjects responded Yes / 10 subjects responded No.
- 57% were in Little League, and 15% were not.
- Play Sandlot Baseball: 28 Yes / 12 No
- 70% played sandlot baseball / 30% did not.

Age 12: 46 Respondents

- Playing in Little League: 14 yes / 32 subjects responded No.
- 30% were in Little League and 70% were not.
- Play Sandlot Baseball: 27 yes / 19 subjects responded No.
- Play Sandlot Baseball: 58% yes / 42% responded No.

Age 13: 55 Respondents

- Playing in Little League: 9 Yes / 46 responded No.
- 16% were in Little League, and 83% were not.
- Play Sandlot Baseball: 44 yes / 11 No.
- Play Sandlot Baseball: 80% yes/ 20% responded No.

Lessons from the survey and data from National Adolescent Health Organizations:

The alarm is sounding loud. The transition from childhood to early adolescence is a struggle. Kids are faced with the crossroad map. They have the option of taking multiple avenues and directions in mapping their future paths or fates.

One path is to be socially active in groups that are constructive, others destructive and criminal, while some may opt to socially isolate.

The survey suggested the idea that most teenagers at age 13 may dismiss structured team play but be socially active in unstructured play or activities. This lends credence that peers play a more active role in childhood associations and thoughts, leading to various forms of behavioral outlets.

These outlets: Some adolescents may consider a sport that they want to play, others may pursue educational or artistic activities, while others may simply hang out at a local street corner using drugs, street fighting, joining a gang, and robbing. Some may simply check out into their rooms to join cyberchats and other social media forums.

The paths described facing youths is not a novel idea. It's an issue that has been discussed over multiple decades.

The latest data and the study only reinforce that the problem still exists and is increasing, especially since more avenues of individual and social activities are evolving in cyberspace rather than on ball fields.

The consensus over the years is that adolescents need a place to go to express themselves and be social and creative.

CHAPTER 10

CHOOSING ACADEMICS, SPORTS, OR BOTH

A question widely seen as a concern among parents and guardians is, "Does a kid have to choose between playing sports and focusing on academics?"

For many years, parents and educators have disagreed on whether children should prioritize their academics or athletics. While it is true that both athletics and academics are crucial for a child's growth, others contend that they may compete for a child's time and attention, forcing them to make a difficult decision. Research studies, however, indicate that the connection between sports and academics is more nuanced than previously believed and that a child's achievement in sports may even improve their academic performance.

According to a study published in the Journal of School Health, middle school kids who participated in school athletics had higher GPAs and better attendance than those who did not. The survey also discovered that students who played sports were more likely to finish high school and enroll in college. This shows that engaging in athletic activity may benefit academic performance.

Another study indicated that high school athletes were less likely to engage in dangerous habits like smoking, drinking, and drug use. This study was published in the Journal of Adolescent Health. The study also discovered that involvement in sports was linked to improved mental health and higher levels of self-worth. This implies that participation in sports can improve a child's general well-being, which can enhance their academic achievement.

Additionally, studies have demonstrated a favorable relationship between physical activity and cognitive function. According to a study published in the Journal of Pediatrics, children who participated in regular physical activity had greater cognitive performance than those who did not. This shows that playing sports, which entails regular exercise, can actually improve a child's academic achievement by enhancing their cognitive function.

The connection between athletics and academics is not always clear-cut. High school athletes had higher GPAs than non-athletes, but after accounting for other variables, including gender and socioeconomic status, the difference was not statistically significant, as per a study published in the Journal of Educational Psychology. Due to the time and effort needed for practice and competition, some research has also suggested that engaging in high-level sports may have a detrimental effect on academic success.

So, must a child choose between pursuing their academic goals and participating in sports? No, I don't believe so. While it is true that sports and academics may vie for a child's time and focus, research indicates that involvement in sports may actually improve a child's academic achievement and general well-being. Sports may also help kids develop valuable life skills like teamwork, leadership, and time management, which can help them on and off the pitch.

How can a balance be maintained between academics and sports?

One way to maintain this balance is through time management. By fostering solid time management skills and making sure that sports engagement does not conflict with homework and study time, parents and educators can encourage a child's participation in sports while simultaneously placing a high priority on academic accomplishment. Children should also learn to prioritize their activities and allocate time for both academics and sports.

Another way to maintain balance is by setting realistic goals. Children should set goals for both academics and sports and work towards achieving them. It is essential to set achievable goals as this will help build self-confidence and motivate them to continue pursuing both academics and sports.

Additionally, parents and coaches should encourage children to take breaks and rest when needed. Rest is essential for physical and mental recovery, which can improve both academic and sports performance. Children who do not get enough rest may feel fatigued and have difficulty concentrating, which can negatively impact their academic performance.

It is also important to note that children should be encouraged to pursue sports that interest them. This will make it easier for them to stay motivated and committed to both academics and sports. Children who participate in sports that they do not enjoy may lose interest and become less motivated, which can negatively impact their academic performance.

Furthermore, parents and coaches should emphasize the importance of sportsmanship and teamwork. Children who participate in sports are likely to develop important life skills such as teamwork, leadership, and communication. These skills can also have a positive impact on academic performance. By providing after-school sports programs and academic support services, schools can also contribute to the promotion of both academics and athletics.

In conclusion, scientific evidence indicates that sports engagement may benefit a child's academic success and general well-being. While a child's time and attention may be divided between athletics and academics, this does not mean that they are incompatible pursuits. As long as academic success is given preference, parents, teachers, and schools can promote a child's engagement in sports while also encouraging intellectual success. The research suggests that a youngster can pursue both academics and athletics, and that both can be advantageous for their growth.

CHAPTER 11

SANDLOT BASEBALL IN LATIN AMERICA AND A TICKET TO CLIMBING OUT OF POVERTY

Sandlot baseball, also known as pick-up baseball, is a popular informal version of the sport in America that is played by kids of all ages in neighborhoods and parks across the country. Unlike organized leagues, sandlot baseball has no coaches, uniforms, or structured games. It is simply a game played for fun and to develop skills.

One of the reasons for the popularity of sandlot baseball among kids in America is its accessibility. Unlike organized leagues, which often require expensive equipment and registration fees, sandlot baseball requires nothing more than a bat, a ball, and a few friends. This means that kids from all backgrounds can participate and enjoy the sport. The freedom that comes with sandlot baseball is another reason why it's always been fairly popular among kids. Without coaches or parents supervising, kids are free to create their own rules and play the game in their own way. This leads to creative variations of the game and a sense of ownership over the sport. This also provides an opportunity for kids to socialize and build relationships with others in their community. By playing pick-up games with other kids in the neighborhood, kids can develop friendships and connections that extend beyond the baseball diamond. This sense of community can be particularly important for kids who may feel isolated or disconnected from their peers.

According to a survey conducted by the Aspen Institute, 30% of children in America ages 6-12 participated in an organized baseball league in 2018, but an additional 15% played baseball informally with friends and family. This suggests that sandlot baseball is still a popular form of sport among kids in America.

One example of the enduring popularity of sandlot baseball is the annual National Sandlot Tournament, which is held in Hartford, Connecticut. The tournament, which was started in 2016, brings together teams of kids from around the country to compete in a weekend-long event. The tournament emphasizes the fun and community-building aspects of sandlot baseball, and has attracted teams from as far away as California and Texas.

How Sandlot Baseball Contributes Towards Poverty Alleviation

Sandlot Baseball has served as a ticket for many children and adolescents to climb out of poverty. The informal nature of sandlot baseball means that it is accessible to all, regardless of socioeconomic status, and provides an opportunity for young people to develop their skills, build relationships, and gain a sense of purpose and identity. In this discussion, we will explore how sandlot baseball has helped many young people in Latin America to overcome poverty and achieve success.

According to a report by the United Nations Development Programme (UNDP), Latin America is the most unequal region in the world, with nearly one third of its population living in poverty. For many young people in this region, poverty means limited access to education, healthcare, and other basic needs, which can lead to a lack of opportunities and a sense of hopelessness. However, sandlot baseball provides a pathway out of poverty for many of these young people.

One of the ways that sandlot baseball can help young people in Latin America to break the shackles of poverty is by providing a sense of community and belonging. In many communities, sandlot baseball is a way of life, and it brings people together across generations and social classes. By participating in sandlot baseball, young people can build relationships with others who share their love of the sport, and this sense of community can provide a support system that helps them to overcome the challenges of poverty.

Another way that sandlot baseball can financially help adolescents in Latin America is by providing a pathway to professional baseball. Many of the best baseball players in the world have come from Latin America, including legends like Roberto Clemente and David Ortiz. For young people who dream of playing professional baseball, sandlot baseball provides a platform to showcase their talents and catch the attention of scouts and coaches.

For example, Carlos Correa, a Puerto Rican professional baseball player, started playing sandlot baseball when he was just four years old. He went on to play for his high school team and then for the Puerto Rican national team, before being drafted by the Houston Astros in 2012. Today, Correa is one of the best shortstops in Major League Baseball, and he credits his success to his early experiences playing sandlot baseball.

Apart from providing a pathway to professional baseball, sandlot baseball can also develop important life skills that can help them to succeed in other areas of their lives. For instance, playing sandlot baseball requires discipline, teamwork, and perseverance, all of which are essential qualities for success in any field. By developing these skills through sandlot baseball, young people can gain a sense of confidence that can help them to overcome the challenges of poverty.

According to a report by ESPN, many Major League Baseball players from Latin America credit their success to their experiences playing sandlot baseball. For instance, Dominican Republic native Nelson Cruz, who is one of the most successful players in the league, said in an interview, "I learned everything I know about baseball on the streets. Playing on the streets was what made me who I am today."

In conclusion, sandlot baseball has played an important role in helping many young people in Latin America to climb out of poverty. By providing a sense of community, a pathway to professional baseball, and an opportunity to develop important life skills, sandlot baseball has helped many young people to overcome the challenges of poverty and achieve success. As Carlos Correa said in an interview with ESPN, "Baseball can change lives. It did for me, and it can for others too."

CHAPTER 12

DREAM TO THE MAJOR LEAGUES

We all have dreams. Dreams are intrinsic to the nourishment of cognitive rejuvenation. We experience Rapid Eye Movements (REM) sleep every night. During the REM stage of the sleep cycle, our minds are refreshed, and we create dreams. Dreams help us to explore our inner thoughts and feelings. They give meaning to our lives, offer insight into our past experiences, reveal our deep-rooted conflicts, stimulate our inner passions, and visualize our future.

For some, dreams offer a life of imagination where we can pretend who we want to become. We are active participants in symbolic images that speak to our consciousness through our unconscious thoughts. Fantasies come alive. There are no restrictions, no thoughts regarding our incapabilities, and no ideas that tell us we cannot be who we want to be. It offers the spirit needed to energize who we are as individuals. It is an exhilarating experience to fulfill a dream.

For some, the dream of playing in the backyard with family or friends, being included in a sandlot game, and being chosen to play on an organized team is a dream of a lifetime for a child athlete.

For a very select few, playing baseball as a youngster and making it to the Major Leagues, like The Big Show, is the ultimate athletic dream turned into reality. This elite group of athletes master the various stages of athletic maturation. They begin with an awareness of the game and work hard to perfect the skills required to compete in professional baseball. Some of us would trade our present vocations in a flash to have a chance to play in the cleats of a Major Leaguer.

But how do major league players make it to the big leagues? Several players were interviewed to establish their road to the major leagues. What factors spark their interest in baseball? What propels them to make their dream come true? What lessons can they offer us from their experiences?

When a baseball fan thinks of the classic sandlot player, Lawrence Peter "Yogi" Berra comes to mind. Raised in the Hill section of Saint Louis, Missouri, Yogi played sandlot ball on the streets of this bluecollar neighborhood with kids that shared his passion for baseball, including a future big leaguer, Joe Garagiola.

Physically, Yogi was an atypical-looking player for the big leagues. He was about 5'8" with a broad physique compared to stereotypical players who are usually tall, slender, and agile. Despite his physical makeup, Yogi played in 10 World Series as a New York Yankee. He was the catcher of the first and only perfect no-hit game in a World Series and also shared the Yankee locker room with iconic teammates, such as Joe DiMaggio, Mickey Mantle, and Whitey Ford. He later managed the New York Yankees and Mets to the World Series. Yogi's words of wisdom are frequently referred to in books, magazines, and on television as "Yogi-isms." His career was honored with an induction to The Baseball Hall of Fame in Cooperstown, New York, in 1973.

As a tribute to Yogi's amazing career, a museum and learning center located in Little Falls, New Jersey, bears his name. Yogi and the director of the museum responded to my inquiry regarding his thoughts on sandlot baseball and shared an insight on free-style play.

UNRESTRAINED CREATIVITY

Feb. 4, 2002

Dear Dr. Zysman:

Mr. Berra passed along your request to me, as we are both pleased that you are devoting a project to helping children, using baseball as a vehicle. I am director of the Yogi Berra Museum & Learning Center, whose mission is education (see enclosed brochure) and co-author of his recent book, "When You Come to a Fork in the Road, Take It!" I can tell you that Mr. Berra, in fact, shares some of your cogent observations.

In answering your questionnaire, Mr. Berra responded thusly:
1) We played whatever was in season, soccer, football, softball, baseball, even roller hockey. Baseball was the longest season and we built our own field out of an old garbage dump on The Hill. We just had fun playing among themselves, choosing sides. I think it's important kids don't just concentrate on one sport, but to play as many as they can.

2) My first organized teams was the Stags AC, part of a YMCA league, when I was 12 or 13. But it was really a neighborhood team; we organized and managed ourselves. The Y just provided the T-shirts.

3) The big thing is we loved to play. We devised games to help our coordination - corkball - or hitting a small object with a broomstick. That helped teach me you don't have to swing hard to hit it hard. Plus we refereed ourselves so we always got along. By developing a love for sports, you develop a desire to improve.
I always wanted to get better and did whatever I could - especially listening to others, like Bill Dickey when I was just coming up with the Yankees. If you work hard and really dedicate yourself to something, there's no telling what you can achieve.

4) Baseball was the game I liked best; for one thing, your size didn't matter. And I was short. We all got along, we played every position, and just had fun playing.

5) I think the games are too organized - I mean too much parental involvement. The big thing is that you don't see kids playing every day, on their own. They have lots of other distractions - computers, video games and all that stuff. And even their playing is too organized - we never had what they call "play dates." We just played - simple as that.

Best of luck with your book, and I do hope you'll consider supporting the Museum - Mr. Berra is dedicated to helping others, and wants kids to get the most out of their childhood, just like he did.

Sincerely,

Dave Kaplan
Director

Thomas "Tommy" Lasorda was a pitcher for the Brooklyn Dodgers, sometimes referred to as ("DEM BUMS"). They are historically known for breaking the major league color barrier in 1947 by recruiting Jackie Robinson to join the team.

The Dodgers were a successful National League team who, however, often fell short of winning a World Championship to their arch-New York American League rivals, The Yankees. Finally, they beat the Yankees in the 1955 World Series. Following the 1957 season, to the dismay of many Brooklynites, the Dodgers moved to Los Angeles, California.

Tommy went on to manage the Los Angeles Dodgers between 1976-1996, led his team to two World Series titles (1981 and 1988) as well as managed the United States National Team 2000 Olympics baseball team in Sydney, Australia.

Tommy was inducted for his accomplishments to the Baseball Hall of Fame in 1997. His plaque highlights his accomplishments as a proud lifelong member of the Dodger Organization. Tommy, like so many other kids, developed a passion for baseball, an instinct to win which evolved into fabled adult life in the game.

Unrestrained Creativity

He writes:

Response Page

Respondent's Name:

I became interest in baseball when I was in the second or third grade. ~~grade~~

When I was in junior high was the first time I played for an organized team, I played on our neighborhood team when I was in the 3rd grade — where I grew up we didn't have little league, or Babe Ruth league, or american legion —

When I started to play competitive baseball, I wanted to win real bad. that carried into professional baseball.

I believe all youngsters should play baseball as it teaches them good habits, that will help them in life.

Tom Lasorda

Unrestrained Creativity

In 1951, a baseball was hit that was heard around the world. The New York Giants beat the National League favorites, the Brooklyn Dodgers, in a losers go-home season playoff game. The winning walk-off homerun jettisoned off the bat of Bobbie Thompson against the Dodger pitcher, Ralph Brancha. The winner went on to the World Series to face the New York Yankees. The Thompson homerun is permanently embedded in the annals of baseball history.

I had the pleasure of interviewing Bobbie Thompson by telephone in 2002 after he responded to my written request to learn about the origins of his interest in baseball and his thoughts on how kids should evolve in learning, later appreciating the sport.

The interview lasted slightly over an hour. For a player who was often a topic of discussion on sports broadcasts and whose homerun is replayed repeatedly during playoff season, Mr. Thompson discussed his famed moment with great humility. For example, he cited frequent encounters by neighborhood residents at a grocery checkout in his hometown at the time in Watchung, New Jersey. When asked about his historic moment, he responded that it was a lucky shot while doing his job.

Thompson's evolution into baseball had simple roots. He played catch in the backyard of his Staten Island Home with his brother, a customary beginning of an athletic youth in his era. He later played semi-pro baseball while in the military during World War II. He mentioned that he was not overly zealous about baseball, but he enjoyed sports in general. Given his career statistics, he was obviously a terrific baseball player.

Consistent with his personal demeanor and downplaying his place in baseball history, Thompson's message was direct and clear. He believed that young athletes need to play baseball and all sports for fun. His belief was that exploration and growth came from the spontaneity of playing. Over-structuring play was a potential deterrent in inspiring children from enjoying each other and baseball.

Thompson concluded the interview with great pride when speaking of his experiences with the New York Giants and the Milwaukee Braves. He was honored in being followed by two legendary players: Willie Mays and Hank Aaron. Mays, a rookie with the Giants, was on deck when Thompson hit his home run. Later as a Milwaukee Brave, he took pride in saying that his ankle injury, which resulted from a slide into second base, gave rise to Henry Aaron, his replacement. Aaron and Mays became two of the greatest home run hitters in baseball history, and both were inducted into the Hall of Fame in Cooperstown.

Even if Thompson is not enshrined in the renowned plaque room gallery, the artifacts of his illustrious career are forever showcased in the Hall of Fame.

After Thompson described his unique playing days, we jokingly concluded our chat with me saying, "Mr. Thompson, you are without a doubt the center of historical moments."

Several years ago, I had face-to-face interviews with 2-star players for the New York Mets, Bud Harrelson and Jon Matlack.

Both Harrelson and Matlack played as Mets in the 1973 World Series. Harrelson played shortstop, and Matlack was a starting pitcher.

Harrelson also played for the famed 1969 World Championship Mets - a team never expected to be in the World Series and was certainly an unfathomable surprise in beating the mighty invincible Baltimore Orioles. That loveable surprising Mets team has been referred to as the "Amazin Mets" and the "Miracle Mets." In the 1977 movie "OH GOD," the comedian George Burns, playing the almighty, states, "the last miracle I did was the 1969 Mets."

It was a cold January morning when I met with Bud Harrelson in his office at the Long Island Ducks complex in Central Islip, New York. Bud was part owner and the first manager of a newly formed Independent Minor League team. This followed years of him playing, coaching, and managing for the New York Mets. Bud was a very down-to-earth and gracious man who was very forthcoming in his responses to my inquiry.

He began the interview by recalling his early days of playing with his brother on a team that his father volunteered to coach. I also played not only with my brother but with other guys. No real pressure or expectations; the real premise was to go to a ballpark or a school yard playing baseball.

Like Yogi Berra, Bud was not a prototypical physical player who was commonly scouted for the major leagues. "I was a snoot nose runt that had some ability to play, and I probably over-practiced as a kid. I mean, it was always a ball glove." He overcame the reference of being the "little guy" with his desire to play and be creative enough to fit in. He played many other sports to have fun with friends, but he proudly claimed, "I always played baseball."

When first asked about his thoughts on coaching, he cited an example that his son had as a 9-year-old with a coach who was demanding, critical, and judgmental. This coach's desire to produce miniature Met and Yankee players overshadowed the fun of playing. For this coach, the child athlete had to take baseball too seriously, a phase in the child's development where simply playing is more important than winning and mastering the sport.

Bud conceived the sandlot experience as trying to "put as many kids together, as that's what sandlot is all about." All the kids "knew each other, played with another sandlot group of guys living three blocks away, and they put the teams against each other… You have a couple of balls, a couple of bats, no one had helmets, and you went down and played."

As per changing times, kids have many options nowadays deciding how to spend their time. But in yesteryear, referred by Bud as "the old stickball days," kids used "walls at schools, played on concrete, play on the blacktop, anything you could find." These makeshift playing venues took the fear out of playing and even created some great hitters, such as "Joe Torre." The aim was to be with others in a friendly competition.

Creativity, Bud emphasized, led to learning and reduced performance anxiety, where making mistakes and errors were acceptable. As a prevailing message, he believed that kids need to just play, make their mistakes, and not be overcoached or pressured by their parents to perform at a level prematurely.

As a Major League player, Bud readily admitted that he made mistakes that were inherent in the game.

Toward the conclusion of the interview, he shared a story. Despite being an accomplished baseball player, he often threw baseballs against the wall in his basement. "I was using my arm and reacting to the ball coming off the wall." Playing is about the player's determination, desire, and practice. It was this unwavering commitment, creativity, and self-determination that led Bud to make the big leagues, enjoy the privilege of managing in the Major Leagues and achieve the ultimate passion of owning a professional baseball team.

I met Jon Matlack on a frigid winter evening in Oneonta, New York. I invited him to dinner at a once well-known family restaurant in the area, Christophers. The atmosphere was rustic, which fit Jon's easy casual style and gracious, benevolent manner. He told his story and shared his insights:

Like many other players, Jon Matlack started playing baseball at a very early age. Beginning with his dad at age 3, he later played for a loosely organized little league team. He loved to play to connect with others, and when alone, he threw baseballs at tin cans. The object was to play and be himself with his own style.

Unrestrained Creativity

Jon entered professional baseball at the age of 17. Over the years as a player and later coach, he presented some interesting insights into the maturation of a professional player.

One of his main points was that players "need to take risks, accept challenges, and take responsibility for their play." Experiencing and accepting failure is part of the learning process.

Another key point here was the will to accept challenges. A player that is not challenged is one who does not learn. Overcoaching thwarts creativity and learning.

The sandlot experience, especially experienced today by the emerging Latin American players, is an internally driven passion coupled with a strong attitude for wanting to play baseball over an expectation by someone outside of themselves.

Jon's takeaway message that I gathered from the session was to allow the player to establish their own individual style in achieving their goals as opposed to dictating how they should perform. Simply put, let the players be creative in establishing an individualistic style of play that would ultimately lead to success.

The comments and thoughts presented by these highly successful players interviewed convey a prevailing theme.

Spontaneous play is rooted in the beginnings of their careers. They found creative means of playing baseball for the sake of having fun and forming friendships.

Their passion and love for the game evolved beyond the course of just playing baseball. They often played many sports. They encouraged that path in developing child athletes. Each sport fine-tunes athletic skills, which are applied later to baseball mastery. Upon researching the biography of many professional baseball players, one learns that they were proficient in multiple sports and could have played professional football, basketball, and soccer, amongst others. In fact, some great baseball players were initially interested in other sports and eventually chose baseball in their later adolescence.

Another important message to parents and coaches is to let kids play naturally. Do not superimpose personal expectations onto the young athletes. Let them make mistakes, which is a part of the game.

Avoid living vicariously through the child but live with the child athlete by encouraging and supporting them. Creativity emanates from trial and error. Conformity arrives from rigidity and over-structuring, which may lead to dropping out.

In a nutshell, uninhibited play, commensurate with the experimentation and creativity phase, is critical in child development. It is also significant in the process of forming a child's identity, self-perception, and self-esteem. Let kids be kids. Let them play ball. Let them be themselves on and off the field.

From resilience and teamwork to leadership and discipline, let baseball be a game that builds myriads of skills for your child.

CHAPTER 13

FOUL BALL: PARENTS PLAYING BEHIND THE FOUL LINE

Parents are great fans. The child athletes welcome the presence of parents, grandparents, and other family members attending their games. They feel encouraged and supported. Their self-esteem is bolstered. It enhances their interest in playing their best and many look forward to stopping at their favorite ice cream stand at the end of the game. It's a thrill and a treat.

The presence of a parent can also be an unpleasant experience that invites pressure on the child athlete that depletes the excitement of being with teammates and playing for fun. Examine the case of James:

James is an 11-year-old little league player. On his scheduled games, James wakes up eagerly to dress up in his team uniform. He eats a quick breakfast, and plays out some practice throws as he waits for his father, Allen (AL), to drive him to the field. In the car, AL tells Jimmy that he is a star player and expects him to do well. AL is generally demanding of Jimmy and the father's expectation was well heeded. Jimmy finally arrives at the field and the goal was not limited to playing baseball and having fun but was now seeking to please his father.

AL has added pressure on Jimmy. AL once fantasized that he would play professional baseball. He injured his rotator cuff playing High School baseball which permanently upset his aspirations.

Years later, AL was elated when his son took an interest in baseball and showed some talent. AL began to dream that his son would be awarded a college scholarship and later be drafted by a major league baseball organization.

However, the protagonist in the dream was not Jimmy, but the father. AL was vicariously playing out his hopes through his son's play. The behavioral manifestation of AL's personal shattered hopes at the game was overbearing and embarrassing to his son. AL would demand that the team coach play his son in certain positions, and place him at a particular spot in the lineup and if the coach disagreed, an argument ensued.

While Jimmy was at bat, AL would shout to him every now and then, "You must get a hit." "Better not strikeout." "The game is on the line."

When the umpire called strike 2, AL's responded, "It was clearly a ball. You are blind UMP. Go Home."

AL was being a micro-manager, micro-ump, and micro-player sitting on the bleachers watching his son play from afar. Emotionally, he was narcissistically connected with the game and showed a lack of empathy for his son. His son was embarrassed, and his teammates sensed his shame.

Jimmy's team lost the game. AL's approach to his son's loss was to criticize him as a means of improving his performance at the next game. AL refrained from using words of encouragement like, "Maybe we can do better next time. You played the best you could today." Instead, AL scolded the son's play and made him feel that he performed sub- standardly. Jimmy felt depressed, anxious, and emotionally depleted. Fun turned into personal disappointment and misery. Jimmy was secretly hoping that his father would stay home for the next game.

Jimmy's story is becoming commonplace. Parents are interfering in the games by their over-involvement. They have difficulty separating from the child athlete to the extent that their son or daughter is playing for their pleasure as opposed to their own fun. The initial goal of learning comradeship and sportsmanship that is associated with sports is spoiled with displays of parental un-sportsmanly conduct. The child athlete internalizes this behavior and will feel that it's proper to act out on the field. A mixed message; antithetical to the spirit of baseball and sports, in general.

Many trained coaches will teach their players that learning the fundamentals of the sport is key to good play and that staying healthy avoids long-term injury. A developing player, especially a pitcher, should gradually develop arm and leg strength which leads to enhancing velocity and throwing accurately to home plate. Coaches will emphasize to simply throwing fast balls as opposed to experimenting with curve balls, sliders, and other "fancy pitches." A child who prematurely throws a variety of pitches may damage ligaments and muscles that may permanently end their baseball career.

In my own experience, I faced a pitcher who had one of the sharpest breaking curve balls I have ever seen. His ball would travel at my hips, I would veer backwards and then it abruptly curved over the plate for a called strike. I often thought he was Sandy Koufax's protégé. Koufax played for the Los Angeles Dodgers, Hall of Famer as of 1973, and was known for his unhittable curves. By the call of strike three, I felt like a fool as did many of my teammates facing Timmy.

However, toward the latter part of the season, Timmy, strained his elbow and made several efforts to return to the mound. He could only throw the so-called fast balls at moderate speed to the middle of the plate which appeared like a big beach ball, and we had a hitting frenzy.

Timmy eventually lost interest in playing, perhaps never pitched again. His father, who often came to the game, was very disappointed since he pitched in his childhood. The father was often seen prior to Timmy's game showing him the art of the grip that spun the ball to curve, and they practiced on the side of the field. Unfortunately for Timmy, the father's perhaps well-intentioned over-involvement and premature expectation to become a "Koufax" turned out to be harmful. It led to the end of Timmy's playing days and time away from all of us.

Parental interference in a child athlete's play can disrupt the natural maturation process and have detrimental effects on their emotional and physical development. When parents place excessive pressure on their child athlete to perform beyond their age appropriate abilities, it can lead to severe adverse consequences.

Physically, pushing a child to compete at a level that surpasses their physical capabilities can increase the risk of muscular-skeletal injuries. Young bodies are still growing and developing and subjecting them to intense training or competition that exceeds their natural progression can strain their muscles, bones, and joints. This can result in overuse injuries, stress fractures, or other trauma. While many injuries can heal with proper care and rehabilitation, they may cause significant setbacks and potentially discourage the child from continuing to play sports.

Furthermore, the emotional well-being of the child athlete can be significantly affected by parental pressure. The child may experience increased stress, anxiety, and a diminished sense of enjoyment in the sport. When parents emphasize winning, success, or meeting unrealistic expectations, it can create a high pressure environment that erodes the child's self-confidence and love for the game.

Placing undue pressure on a child athlete may also hinder their overall physical development. Every child progresses at their own pace, and forcing them to perform beyond their abilities may prevent them from developing fundamental skills and techniques properly. It is crucial to allow children to go through the natural maturation process at their own pace, which includes gradually building their physical capabilities and skill sets. This incremental development helps ensure a solid foundation for future growth and can reduce the risk of burnout or quitting sports altogether.

The emotional impact may not be as transient as a physical injury. The child athlete's thought of letting down the parents can surface a host of negative feelings, principally an injured self-esteem. Often parents do not recognize that an emotional reaction from criticism can have long-term effects on a child's mental health. The negative messages received by the child immerses into the unconscious which has longitudinal adverse effects. The child's distorted view of themselves can injure their confidence and performance in sports as well as life in general.

Parental misconduct in amateur sports is a growing phenomenon. Sports writers have documented multiple incidents like these for many years. Even sports psychologists have coined a term for this pattern of behavior. It is referred to as Little League Parent Syndrome (LLPS). These involve parental acting out behaviors related to shouting out foul language at coaches, young players, or umpires.

In some instances, the intensity of unsportsmanlike conduct is turning severe. Parents are jumping out of the bleachers and brawling on the field. For example, in Lakewood Colorado, parents ran onto the field brawling with each other after disagreeing with an Umpire's call. The example of this behavior deflates the player and the team they came to cheer for. It demonstrates poor role models and destructive codes of conduct for any child attending the game, including the players. The primary source of embarrassment is the perpetrators that have difficulty controlling their emotions at a little league game.

Coaches and those organizing team play are pushing back on unruly parental misconduct and addressing the LLPS Syndrome. Umpires have prematurely stopped games and walked off the field. At a game in Newport Harbor, California, the umpire was debased by fans and decided to call the game. The umpire warned parents to stop the taunting before ultimately leaving. Searching the internet will reveal multiple stories on the topic of unsportsmanlike behaviors displayed by parents The message is enough verbal abuse and limits are being imposed. The Game is Over!!

The conduct of parents and family members during youth sports events can greatly influence the experience of the players. By demonstrating good sportsmanship and showing respect for all individuals involved, parents can set a positive example for young athletes in Little League. This aligns with the expectations of Little League for all its participants, including players, coaches, umpires, and volunteers.

The Little League Organization has taken a very strong position as well. The Organization publishes a Parents' Rule of Conduct that clearly delineates parental behaviors and expectations at games.

The rules emphasize that:

1. I will not force my child to participate in sports.

2. I (and my guests) will be a positive role model for my child and encourage sportsmanship by showing respect and courtesy, and by demonstrating positive support for all players, coaches, officials, and spectators at every game, practice, and other sporting event.

3. I (am my guests) will not engage in any kind of unsportsmanlike behavior with any official, coach, player, or parent such as booing or taunting, refusing to shake hands, or using profane language.

4. I will never ridicule or yell at my child or other participants for making a mistake or losing a competition.

5. I will promote the emotional and physical well-being of the athletes ahead of my personal desire I have for my child to win.

6. I will refrain from coaching my child or other players during games and practices unless I am one of the official coaches on the field.

A complete text of the code of conduct can be found at littleleague.org.

When it comes to a child's play, parental over involvement and interference serve minimal value if the intention is solely to demand and control rather than teach or guide. The primary focus should be on creating a pleasant and enjoyable experience for the child athlete. It is essential to recognize that it is their game and allowing them to play to the best of their abilities fosters their growth and development. By encouraging autonomy, fostering a supportive environment, and letting them embrace their own journey, children can truly find joy and fulfillment in their athletic pursuits.

CHAPTER 14

THE HOME OF GENERATIONS

Visualize a home plate in baseball. It takes the form of a pentagon with specific measurements. Its base is 17 inches long, and it has two parallel sides of 16 inches each, converging at a triangular point known as the apex. This shape resembles an A-frame designed house and is commonly referred to as "HOME."

In the game of baseball, home plate holds significant importance and serves various functions. It acts as the central focal point of activity on the field. Positioned between the right-handed and left-handed batter's box, it plays a crucial role in the game's proceedings.

One of the primary functions of home plate is as a meeting place. Prior to each game, team managers, along with umpires, gather at home plate to exchange lineup cards and review the rules. This ritual sets the stage for the game and ensures that all parties involved are on the same page.

The home plate also serves as a venue for special ceremonies and events within the stadium. It is where the stadium announcer may direct fans to join a performer, such as a singer, at home plate to sing the national anthem or engage in a rally chant. This brings together the crowd and creates a sense of unity and enthusiasm before the game begins.

Additionally, home plate is a site for honoring individuals with distinguished accomplishments. Whether it's recognizing a player's milestone achievement, celebrating a retiring player's career, or awarding a player for outstanding performance, home plate holds a symbolic significance in acknowledging excellence within the sport.

During the game, home plate is the base where the pitcher needs to throw the ball partially over to get a called strike. It is the base where the hitter tries to square the barrel of the bat to hit the oncoming ball thrown by the pitcher. It is a place where the pitcher or batter expresses excitement and great disappointment.

The home plate also symbolizes comradeship. When hitting a home run, the player must touch all the bases and Home is the destination. Teammates congratulate with hugs and high-fives when the slugger touches home. Following a game-winning hit, teammates (a.k.a "The Family" as popularized during the 1979 World Series) all gather at home and jump with joy.

Home plate is the site where the game begins and ends.

In our own lives, home is similarly where our day starts and finishes. We wake up with the view of having a productive and rewarding day. Following our daily routines, we come home to communicate, bond, and relax with our families. At the end of an evening, it's a place where we find tranquility, sleep, and create new dreams.

Baseball is a family adventure. With every inning at the ballpark, the player experiences various types of plays on the field which evoke a range of reactions. The ups and downs are also felt by those who spectate the game: parents, grandparents, siblings, and friends with the child athlete. By the end of the game, a collective experience emerges with a great story that bonds everyone involved.

Generally, a player is asked to report their impressions regarding the action that took place on the field. But those rooting for a player and team also have feelings and memories to share, often ladened with potent emotions.

Ann Defilippo attends most games played by her grandsons.

As Ann observed them playing on their respective teams, she was simultaneously linked emotionally with the experience. She wrote:

"I have two grandsons that are passionate about baseball. J.C., 6 years old and J.J., 11 years old. Baseball brings them together. When J.C. is playing J.J., his brother watches him having fun playing with his friends. When J.J. plays, J.C. is in the stands or along the baseline. He gets a huge thrill when he sees his brother at bat or playing the field.

But let me share something special about each grandson that has been most memorable to me and gives me a great thrill talking about the experience. One day I joined my family to watch a game that my son-in-law played with his college buddies. These were players who played college-level baseball, so they were all very good.

At one point during the game, they invited J.C. to come to bat. He had such a grin on his face and physical elation that was precious and forever memorable in my mind. Anyway, they pitched to him and taught him a few baseball techniques, some of those were not familiar to me, and he was now playing confidently with the big guys too.

The day brought indescribable joy to me, for how my young grandson could share a special unforgettable moment with his father, his father's teammates and with me, all which centered around the game of baseball. I am sure that that day will be a topic in our family's memoirs that will exude excitement, laughter and more baseball-sharing moments in the days to come.

As for J.J., baseball is part of his daily life. I observe him walking around his house practicing his batting swing, walking along the shoreline on summer days pretending as if he is playing the field and throwing out a runner trying to go from first to second base.

Actually, J.J. is a pretty good baseball player. He is generally one of the star players on the team and he is often chosen for advanced play leagues. He follows the statistics of his favorite players and is very interested in baseball history.

But I want to share a story that is unique and special. I do not know how many people have experienced this type of child baseball story that plays out a dream. When I watch my grandson at home, he slides on a wood floor as if he is stealing a base during the game. He practices this exercise repeatedly. But he generally does it when he and I are alone in the living room. It's almost as if he is demonstrating a private baseball practice skill only when I am with him. I presume it's his way of sharing a special moment with me as if he is saying, 'Let's keep this between us.'

Well, one day I visited the house, and my daughter tells me about how the living room floor is so worn down that it needs replacement. I believe it was due to my grandson's sliding exercises. I agreed with my daughter, but somehow, I am not sure she knew how the floors were scrapped. I do not think I ever told her, but it's a story that I and my grandson now shares and it revolves around his passion for baseball.

On the field and at home, baseball brings our family together. We watch it on TV, we listen to the Yankees in the car and are all together at the practices and games. Baseball is a major activity in our lives. But for me, it provides bonding and remarkable moments that I can cherish with each of my two young ballplayers."

Joshua Lauria shares that baseball and sports, in general, was lifesaving for him. Josh was raised by his grandparents. His father had minimal involvement with him, and his mother was mentally ill. His grandfather assumed the role of his father and mentored him in sports. The impact his grandfather played on Josh's life and later a mentor who was a friend of the family is heartwarming, tear dropping.

Josh best describes his story in his own words:

My grandfather, Donato Lauria, raised me as his own. My father left me when I was an infant and my mother who is Donato's daughter was diagnosed with mental illness, bipolar schizophrenic, and was incapable of caring for me after she gave birth to me. My grandparents, Donato, and Gloria Lauria raised me since I was 4 months old.

My grandfather was my hero. He taught me sports, showed me stats at a young age, and gave me history lessons about the Brooklyn Dodgers. I became obsessed with baseball, football, and basketball at a very young age. I played Little League Baseball, and I was very good at a very young age. It made my grandfather so proud to watch me play. I hit my first home run at age 11. At the next at-bat, I hit the ball off the fence. I went to my grandfather and said, "Oh man, that was so close it almost went out." He said, "Next at-bat just lower your shoulder just a little bit."

My very next at-bat I did what exactly what he said, and I watched the ball sail over the fence. For my first home run, I was elated and looked at my grandfather like a GOD.

When I was 13 years old, my grandfather had a sudden complication and died from Emphysema. It was so sudden that it shocked us as a family, but for me, my hero was gone, and I was in shambles.

I started playing basketball at the age of 12, a year before my grandfather passed away. At first, I was not very good in the CYO leagues. But I became close friends with Mike and Danny Deutsch. Their father, Mr. John Deutsch (Coach D), coached them in basketball and soccer. Coach D was told that I came from a tough background, tough childhood, and the "good kids from good families" considered me a "hard case."

Mr. D., now my basketball coach, told me during my first practice that I am going to listen, I am going to learn, and I am going to become a ballplayer if he had anything to do with it. His words gave me the confidence to keep working hard even though I knew I was not very good. I didn't get much time on the floor during my first season. I was 13. The season had just began, and I was put in when the game was pretty much decided. My grandfather saw me in two games before he passed away that February. As always, I looked at him in the stands and he gave me a fist pump after grabbing some rebounds and throwing them into the outlet player.

My grandmother made me follow up with my school and sports obligations after my grandfather died. I remember being in practice after he passed and teammates saying to me, "How am I even here after going through that?" I shrugged it off. I didn't really think about it like that. I just thought, hey, my family wants me to keep doing my normal things in life, then I should be here. At night before bed, it would really sink in and I would question if I should be demanding that I don't go to school or to the game I had that week.

I showed up to the next game. We were doing our warmup drills and Coach D. pulled me off the line. "The boys told me what happened. Why did you ever come to the game?" I said it's what my family wants. He looked at me and said, "I can't say that you are ready, but I am going to start you tonight in honor of your grandfather. You're going to go out there and tonight you're going to become a ballplayer. You're going to stick to one guy all game long on defense and you better go out there to make your grandfather proud. He is watching you from above right now..."

In the previous games, I scored maybe 2 or 4 points. On this night, I scored 20 points. At each time the ball went into the hoop, I kept looking up after each hoop and as I was defending this big kid and keeping him away from the boards, being very physical that night, I ran up and down the court wiping my teary eyes, got very emotional thinking about my grandfather. Coach D. noticed my tears and kept giving me a fist pump just like my grandfather did.

At halftime, Coach D. told me "You're giving that kid a rough time and he is their best big man. I told you that you were going to be a ballplayer." I did become a ballplayer that night.

At 13 years of age, my life was in shambles. That moment, that game taught me empathy and selflessness for the rest of my life. Most importantly, I had a father figure that I could rely on in my future.

That day, Coach D. was my hero and role model. I owe him a debt of gratitude for helping change the life of a "hard case." For the rest of that season and seasons beyond, Mr. D. picked me up and dropped me off from each practice and game. As I sit here, I cry my eyes out writing this because Coach D. has just passed from a terminal illness, and I can't imagine where I would be without that man in my life.

Family participation was welcoming in the situations described by Ann and Joshua. They convey a message of encouragement and hope. Baseball, sports in general, was a key component that tied the players to share their passions and heroic moments with their families, especially grandparents. Grandparents and a caring unselfish coach were critical in Josh's youth, in Baseball and Basketball. Ann has taken a very active role in being with her grandsons as they express themselves creatively and play out their dreams through Baseball.

Erik Erickson, the renowned developmental psychologist, argued that the process of aging entails sharing and teaching. He coined this stage as Generativity. Through this process, older individuals pass on their wisdom, accumulated through life experiences, to the younger generations in order to enhance their own sense of purpose and fulfillment in life. This intergenerational exchange serves to enhance older individuals' sense of purpose and fulfillment in life.

Generativity encompasses a deep desire to contribute to the well-being and success of future generations. For child athletes, intergenerational encouragement, support, and love can play a vital role in their personal growth and development. When older individuals take an active interest in the lives of young athletes, they provide a unique perspective and guidance that can be immensely motivating.

Through intergenerational relationships, child athletes have the opportunity to learn from the experiences and insights of older individuals. These interactions can inspire them to overcome challenges, pursue their passions, and develop essential life skills.

The encouragement and support received from older generations can fuel their self-confidence, resilience, and determination.

Moreover, intergenerational connections create a sense of belonging and community for child athletes. Knowing that they have the support and love of older individuals who genuinely care about their well-being can have a profound impact on their overall development. The guidance and mentorship provided by older individuals can foster a strong sense of identity, purpose, and direction in young athletes' lives who may be facing difficult circumstances in their lives. They can learn valuable life skills such as perseverance, resilience, and teamwork, which can benefit them both on and off the playing field.

In turn, the process of generativity brings fulfillment and a sense of meaning to older individuals. By investing in the growth and success of younger generations, they can leave a lasting legacy and positively impact the lives of future leaders and contributors in society.

Parents/guardians should motivate the child athletes as they evolve in their lives with intergenerational encouragement, support, and love.

CHAPTER 15

THE WINDUP

Through the course of this book, we have sojourned through many topics. We explored multiple ideas, given suggestions from professional players, felt the experiences expressed by family members watching their children live the sport they love, heard from amateur players, felt the emotions of a special needs child seeking to fit into a game and now it's time for the windup which ties all these discussions together and brings it home.

The initial premise of the discussion was to explore play and its effects on the development of creativity, self-expression, and self-esteem with the objective of promoting a child's emotional growth as they mature through their developmental years.

There were four phases: Awareness, Knowledge, Experimentation, and Mastery. Each stage is followed sequentially, logically, and emotionally to the next. But there was no assurance at any step beyond awareness that would give the motivation or enthusiasm to reach the mastery stage. An interest in an idea or sport ultimately must have a spark that ignites an excitement within the child that propels them to the mastery stage. Lack of interest may generally lead to dropping out or behaviorally acting out. The flow from Awareness to Mastery extends beyond sports. It has universal applications as it pertains to other subjects and activities in a child s path to adulthood.

Baseball is a sport that is loved by many of us throughout the world. A growing number of children from Latin America, Asia, and Europe are embracing the sport as American kids have done in over 150 years. It served as the stage and scenery in illustrating the underlying theory revealing the influence of play on an individual's childhood.

Baseball is an inclusive sport that contributes to its popularity. A child can play because they want to be part of a group and find enjoyment in being with their peers. Special needs players can partake in baseball.

Baseball invites and accepts players with a wide range of athletic abilities to find a place on the field.

Kids can play in various ways either in Sandlot baseball or in organized Baseball Little League teams.

Baseball also serves to establish character and an esprit de corp. Baseball, especially sandlot play, is a sport that fosters free expression, creativity, group decisions, and individuality. From an emotional perspective, it helps kids from sliding into depression, anxiety, alcohol, and drug addiction and prevents suicide, especially at the beginning of adolescence (age 13) when they tend to drop out of organized leagues and try to find new connections. Baseball can keep them focused on constructive social relationships as opposed to regressing into hanging out on street corners, engaging in anti-social criminal activities or, in some cases, joining street gangs.

Gradually, our culture is substituting outside free play with Artificial Intelligence (AI) technology. This is a trend that is concerning, if not yet, startling. As one scans through the television channels and surfs the internet, there are advertisements that introduce artificial game playing applications. They are marketed as tools for enhancing skills which is a benefit but may lead to social isolation. With some of these AI programs, one can join players from distant places without leaving their homes. This is fine for some kids while for others it serves to avoid face-to-face social interaction.

Social Media further isolates kids from person-to person interaction. Our society has been accustomed to using social media to post our views and share family and memorable photos with those that are closely or peripherally connected to us. In theory, the social media concept was a form of staying connected with those that lived afar, reacquainting with old friends, expressing personal viewpoints, and sharing knowledge.

But over the years since its inception, we have seen a great over-dependency on social media which has led to increased social withdrawal. For kids, social media offers a platform to join secretive groups, be influenced by advertisers of products and games that may be harmful, serve to avoid family gatherings, and distance oneself from going out and playing with other kids. The psycho-bio-social implications of this form of interaction have become so profound that it has become a social disease evolving into pandemic proportions.

Technology was meant to be a tool. It's intriguing to observe a new technologically advanced computer, handheld device, or software application utilized to replace tasks that we consider mundane or unnecessary. It's fascinating to learn how technology can make life easier and offer time to pursue other interests, including family and social time. A historical discovery has gradually been adopted as a substitute rather than an adjunctive aid to enhance our quality of life.

I experienced this development in my field. In the 1980s, I wrote a doctoral dissertation that explored the potential use of information technology as an adjunctive tool in the practice of psychotherapy and specifically with addicted patients. A profession that relied heavily on actual face-to-face interaction, the idea was considered dystonic, unfeasible, and unthinkable at the time. As applications were designed over the past 40 years for psychologists, psychiatrists, and social workers, the idea was embraced and utilized more commonly than the traditional office visits. Now telemedicine and virtual therapy are a mainstay in treatment and appear to become an intrinsic part of practice in the future. Perhaps the mental health community waved an initially unintended goodbye to a practice that prided itself on being and seeing the whole person, in person.

Sport is a microcosm of the greater society. As a trend amongst sports, enthusiasts are communicating in cyber language. They are spinning out data and statistical probabilities and gambling heavily on the potential results from information ascertained from computer-generated analyses. It is not uncommon to see iPhone users rummaging through sports applications to follow the winners and losers in baseball, football, soccer, and other sports.

Unfortunately, they are not watching the actual play on the field.

Even modern baseball stadiums are designed for entertainment and dining. Fans are gathered in stadium clubs and restaurants watching part of a game on television monitors. They are not sitting in stadium seats and following the play-by-play on the field. Some attendees are conducting business and others may be out for an evening at the bar with a spouse or friend. There are more distractions between the stadium attendee and the athletic field action. The universal utilization of the stadiums certainly helps to procure revenue but serves to diminish the basic goal of going to a professional baseball park: watch and root for your team as you immerse into the action.

Tradition and modernization have been in conflict throughout the ages and in every aspect of life. There are factions in every area of human endeavors to maintain orthodox standards of living and those who advocate change, some radical in nature. Both positions offer persuasive arguments. Often the outcome of this organic dialectical process is a middle ground.

Baseball is a sport and currently, society is facing critical decisions regarding technology, autonomy, and the free expression of the human spirit. Simply stated: it's individual freedom versus centralized organization. As discussed in the preceding chapters, the trend has been heading toward structured activities and diminishing self-determination.

Kids naturally grow and express themselves as individuals. While they need encouragement and support from parents, they simultaneously require the freedom to play with others outdoors to learn the skills as well as foster their creative energies. Sandlot baseball, a form of free-style play, has traditionally been an athletic path that includes everyone. It contributes to sound mental and physical health. It's a sport that is thoroughly enjoyed when played. The pitcher walks to the pitching mound, then is given a sign from the catcher, grips the ball to guide it in a desired route, observes the hitter, begins the winds up, releases the ball, and hopes that it sails over home plate for a called strike. The windup refers to the physical technique used by the pitcher for the ball thrown to gain velocity and influence its direction as it travels to home plate.

As the accomplished professional athletes have suggested: Keep playing freely!

Now for the final windup: Visualize the pitcher on the pitching mound. He accepts the sign of the pitch to throw from the catcher who is crouched behind home plate. The pitcher steps on the pitching rubber, lifts his leg, and then strides toward home plate, releasing the ball to fly in its own unique path.

REFERENCES

Abra, Jack, The Motives for Creative Work: An Inquiry with Speculations about Sports and Religion, Hampton Press, Cresskill. New Jersey, 1997.

Adaptive Baseball, Spectrum Television News Story, Binghampton, New York Aired 8/13/2022.

Bengel, Chris, Umpire has Just Enough of the Crowd's Criticism, CBS/MLB Sports, 2017.

Bethel, Dell, Coaching Winning Baseball, Contemporary Book, Chicago, Illinois, 1979.

Bettelheim, Bruno, Love Is Not Enough: The Treatment of Emotionally Disturbed Children. McMillan Publishers, 1967.

Bishop, Christopher and Keth, Kenneth, Psychosocial Stages of Development, Published in Encyclopedia of Cross-Cultural Psychology, 1st edition, pgs 1055-1060, John Wiley & Sons, Inc., 2013.

Braum, Anthony and Deborah Feltz, Effects of Batting Performance: Feedback on Motivational Factors and Batting Performances in Youth Baseball, Perceptual and Motor Skills, pgs. 1367-1378. 1995.

Bretherton, Inge, ed., Symbolic Play, Development of Social Understanding, Academic Press, Orlando, 1984.

Broadus, Catherine: Laughing and Crying with Little League, A Training Manual for Little League Parents, Harper & Row, 1972.

Canfield, Jack, Hansen, Mark V., Donnelly, Mark & Chrissy, Lasorda, Tommy, Chicken Soup for the Baseball Fan's Soul: Inspirational Stories of Baseball, Big-League Dreams and the Game of Life, Health Communications, Inc., Deerfield Beach, Fl., 2001.

Centers for Disease Control and Prevention; https://www.cdc.gov/physicalactivity/index.html

Christopher J. Wretman, School Sports Participation and Academic Achievement in Middle and High School, Society for Social Work and Research, Chicago, 2017.

Cohen, David, The Development of Play, New York University Press, 1987.

Cohen, Sandy, Suicide Rates Among Teen and Young Adults, UCLA Health, March 2022.

Conn, Dennis, Cognition and Creativity, in Introduction to Psychology, Exploration and Applications, St. Paul: West Publishing Co., 1989, pgs.: 1-11.

Cosby, Roger S. and Sawyers, Janet K, Play in the Lives of Children, National Association for the Education of Young Children, Washington, D.C., March 1998.

Dickerson, John, A Behavioral Analysis of Sport, Lupus Books, London, 1976.

Dixon, Ramon, How Far Do You Wanna Go? The True Story of the Man who turned 16 Inner City Kids into a Team of Champions, New Horizon Press, Far Hill. New Jersey, 1997.

Dr. Jayakumar K, Creativity and Athlete Development through Unstructured Play, International Journal for Innovative Research in Multidisciplinary Field, India, 2021.

Edwards, Donald K, Baseball Coaches Complete Handbook, Parker Publishing Company, West Nyack, New York 1966.

Erikson, Joan M., Erikson, Erik, The Life Cycle Completed, W.W. Norton & Co., 1997.

Erickson, Hal, Baseball in The Movies: A Comprehensive Reference, 1915-1991, McFarland Press, Jefferson, North Carolina, 1992.

Figone, AL, Teaching The Mental Aspects of Baseball, A Coache's Handbook, William C. Brown, Dubuque, Iowa, 1991.

Frommer, Harvey: Growing Up at Bat: 50 Years of Little League Baseball, Pharos Books, New York, 1989.

Gent, Peter, The Last Magic Summer: A Season With My Son: A Memoir, W. Morrow Publishing, New York, 1996

Good, Howard, Diamonds in The Dark: America, Baseball and The Movies. Scarelrow Press, Landham, Maryland, 1997.

Haq, Mahbub, Reflections On Human Development Oxford University Press, 1995.

Hinde, Robert, A.J. Clermont- Perret, Nelly, Ann and Hinde, Joan Stevenson, Social Relationships and Cognitive Development: A Fyssen Foundation Symposium, Oxford University Press, New York, 1985.

Kenneth Anderson, Why Addiction Treatment Needs to Be Informed by Natural Recovery Data, American Addiction Centers, 2019.

Kimbro, Dennis, What Makes the Great: Strategies for Extraordinary Achievement, Doubleday Press, New York 1997.

Kindall, Jerry and Winkin, John, eds., The Baseball Coaching Bible, Human Kinetics Publishing, Inc. Champlain, Illinois, 2000.

Ko, S,, An Empirical Analysis of Children's Thinking and Learning in Computer Game Context, Educational Psychology vol. 22 (2), 2002, pps, 219233.

Larson, Reed W., A Psychology of Positive Youth Development, American Psychologist, January, 2000, pgs 170-173.

Lauren J. Tanz, Amanda T. Dinwiddie, Christine L. Mattson, Julie O'Donnell, Nicole L. Davis, Drug Overdose Deaths Among Persons Aged 10–19 Years, Centers for Disease Control and Prevention, 2022.

Leavy, Jane, Sandy Koufax: A Lefty's Legacy, Harpers Collins Publishing, 2002.

Llewellyn, Jack, Ph.D., Let em Play: What Parents, Coaches & Kids Need to Know About Youth Baseball, Longstreet Press, Inc., Marrietta, Georgia, 2001.

Lesyk, Jack J., and Kornspan, Alan, Coach's Expectations and Beliefs Regarding Benefits of Youth Sport Participation, Perceptual and Motor Skills, vol 90, April, 2000, pgs.: 399-402.

Lieberman, J. Nina, Playfulness: Its Relationship to Imagination and Creativity, Academic Press, 1972.

Lindstrand, P., Parents of Children with Disabilities: Evaluate the Importance of Computer in Child Development, Journal of Special Education Technology, 16 (2), 2001, pgs.: 43-52.

Little League Baseball, Inc. South Williamsport, Pennsylvania, www.littleleague.org.

Mahler, Margaret S., Separation- Individuation: The Selected Papers of Margaret S. Mahler, Vol. 2, Rowman and Littlefield Publishers, 1977.

Matthew Harper, Eli Lilly's Mounjaro succeeds in second weight loss study, paving way for FDA review, STAT, 2023.

Moorman, Chick, Lessons in Baseball, pgs. 97-99, in Canfield, Jack, Hanson, Mark Victor and Kimberly Kirberger, Chicken Soup for the Teenage Soul, 101 Stories of Life, Love and Learning, Health Communications, Inc., Deerfield, Florida, 1997.

Nana Wilson Mbabazi Kariisa, Puja Seth, Herschel Smith IV, Nicole L. Davis, Drug and Opioid Involved Overdose Deaths, Centers for Disease Control and Prevention, 2020.

National Alliance of Mental Health, (NAMI), Arlington, Virginia; Nami.org

National Baseball Hall of Fame, Cooperstown, New York: baseballhalloffame.org

National Center for Drug Abuse Statistics (NCDAS) drugabusestatistics.org

National Institute of Drug Abuse; (NIDA): nida.nih.gov

Nolan, E.J., The Day Shay Got to Play, Baseball Almanac, Inc. May, 2017.

Ostrom, T.M. The Sovereignty of Social Cognition, in Wyer, R.S., jr. & Srull, T.K., eds. Handbook of Social Cognition, vol.1 pgs., 1-38, Lawrence Ebron Associates Publishers 1984.

Ozempic, https://www.ozempic.com/

Park, Kelly G., Just Like Me, When the Pros Played on the Sandlot, Sandsbury Press, Inc, Mechanicsburg, PA, 2020.

Parsons, Marcella and Hays Young, Steven, Sandlot Stories, Arose Books, Incline Village, NV, 2003.

Patrick, Helen, Ryan, Allison; Alfred-Liro, Corine; Fredricks, Jennifer; Hruda, Ludmilla & Eccles, Jacquelynne, Journal of Youth and Adolescence, volume 28, No. 6, pgs. 7-41. 1979

Psychosocial Development in Late Adulthood, Hostos Community College Library, Bronx, NY, 2022.

Piaget, Jean, Play, Dreams and Imitations in Childhood, W.W. Norton & Co., 1962.

Piaget, Jean and Inhelder, Barbel, The Psychology of the Child, Basic Books, 1969.

Piers, Maria W, ed., Play and Development Piaget, Jean, Wolf, Peter, Spitz, Renee, Lorenz, Konrad, Barkley, Lois and Erikson, Erik, Play Development: A Symposium., pps, 119-126, W.W. Norton and Company, 1972.

Pressure and Youth Sports Study, Yellow book, posted on Yellowbookprogram.com, April 7, 2017.

Project Play Summit, 2022. The Aspen Institute, Washington, DC.

Ringolsby, Tracy, Ryan's Hope: Thanks to Hall of Fame Determination, Nolan Ryan Went from Thrower to Pitcher Over 27 Amazing Seasons, Memories and Dreams, 8, Winter 2022, Magazine of The Baseball Hall of Fame, pgs. 36-38

US Dept. of Health and Human Services, https://www.hhs.gov/

Seymour, Harold, Baseball: The People's Game, Oxford University Press, New York, 1990.

Singer, Dorothy, Ed.d., Olfman, Sharna, Ph.D. Helix, Jane, Ph.D., Presentation "Crisis of Technologies and Demise of Play. Presented at the American Psychological Association Conference, August, 2003.

Singer, Jerome, The Child's World of Make Believe, Academic Press, 1973.

Singer, J.L., Imaginative Play and Adaptive Development, (pgs. 6-26) in Goldstien, J.H., ed. Toys, Play and Development, Cambridge University Press, 1994.

Smith, Ronald and Smoll, Frank, Self Esteem and Children's Reactions to Youth Sport Coaching Behaviors: A Field Study of Self Enhancement processes, Developmental Psychology, vol.26, No.6, pgs. 987-993, 1990.

Special Olympics, Special Olympics.org.

Stepka, Barbara, Teens in Trouble, Parents of High Schoolers and Young Adults Confront a Growing Mental Health Crisis, The AARP Magazine, vol.65, No.5A, August/September, 2022, pgs.: 33-34.

Susan F. Tapert, Lisa Caldwell, Christina Burke, Alcohol and the Adolescent Brain—Human Studies, National Institute on Alcohol Abuse and Alcoholism, https://pubs.niaaa.nih.gov/

Syer, John, Team Spirit: The Elusive Experience, Kingwood, London, 1986.

Tanz, LJ, Dinwiddle, AT, Mattson, CL, Odonnell, J, Davis, NL, Drug Overdose Deaths Among Persons Aged 10-19 Years- United States, July, 2019December, 2021 MMWR Morb Mortal Wkly Rep 2022, 71: 1576-1582.

The Americans with Disabilities Act (1990), U.S. Department of Justice, Civil Rights Division, www.ada.gov.

Towle, Sean, Reporter, Channel 7 News, Denver, Co, Westgate Elementary School Parents Brawling Each Other, Lakewood, Colorado June, 2019.

Van Auken, Lance, Play Ball: The Story of Little League Baseball, Penn State University Press, University Park, PA, 2001.

Verenikina, Irna, Herrington, Jan, Peterson, Robert, Montel, Jessica, Journal of Interactive Learning Research, 21 (1), Pgs: 139-159. 2010

Winnicott, D.W. Playing and Reality, Routledge Publications, 1982.

Wilken, Kendall, Competing with Class, The Baseball Coaching Bible, Pgs.,20-30,

Wolff, Rick, The Psychology of Winning Baseball: A Coach's Handbook, Parker Publications, West Nyack, New York, 1986

Yogi Berra Museum & Learning Center, Little Falls, New Jersey: yogiberramuseam.org

ABOUT THE AUTHOR

Dr. Shafer H. Zysman is the author of "Unrestrained Creativity-How Sandlot Baseball Can Unleash Creativity for Kids in the Tech Age." – a book that reflects upon the significance of how children use sports as a social means to foster creativity and self-esteem and develop individual identities.

Dr. Zysman has been in practice for over 40 years in the areas of Psychoanalytic Psychotherapy, Alcohol / Substance Abuse Treatment, Behavioral Health Treatment with patients ranging in ages from childhood to the elderly. He was also involved in creating and administering programs that have helped a multitude of patients suffering from mental illness and alcohol/drug Addiction.

Dr. Zysman graduated from University at Buffalo, Ohio University and Adelphi University with degrees in multiple academic disciplines.

www.ingramcontent.com/pod-product-compliance
Lightning Source LLC
LaVergne TN
LVHW041704070526
838199LV00045B/1200